Articulate Storyline Essentials

Discover Articulate Storyline's ability to enhance your e-learning by allowing you to create engaging and interactive stories

Ashley Chiasson

BIRMINGHAM - MUMBAI

D1127219

Articulate Storyline Essentials

Copyright © 2015 Packt Publishing

First published: March 2015

Production reference: 1050315

Published by Packt Publishing Ltd.
Livery Place
35 Livery Street
Birmingham B3 2PB, UK.

ISBN 978-1-78439-207-9

www.packtpub.com

Credits

Author
Ashley Chiasson

Reviewers
Asma Shaikh
Farhaan Shaikh
Amit Kumar Soni
Helen Tyson

Commissioning Editor
Edward Bowkett

Acquisition Editor
Rebecca Youé

Content Development Editor
Sriram Neelakantan

Technical Editor
Subin Cherian

Copy Editors
Karuna Narayanan
Laxmi Subramanian

Project Coordinator
Judie Jose

Proofreaders
Simran Bhogal
Paul Hindle

Indexer
Monica Ajmera Mehta

Production Coordinator
Arvindkumar Gupta

Cover Work
Arvindkumar Gupta

About the Author

Ashley Chiasson is an instructional designer and consultant with nearly a decade of experience developing high-quality e-learning solutions for various clients. She holds a master's of education (post-secondary studies) and a bachelor of arts (linguistics and psychology). In addition to being a small business owner, Ashley works for Mount Saint Vincent University, Canada, as their resident instructional developer. As a self-proclaimed ambassador of the Articulate software, Ashley truly believes that the only thing standing between you and your ability to create engaging and interactive e-learning projects is your imagination.

With a strong belief of creating her own professional freedom, Ashley has become a successful entrepreneur, working hard to find a place for herself in the big world of e-learning. She works hard to ensure that her clients are satisfied, because without them, entrepreneurship would be a lonely place.

This book is the first of many for Ashley, and she has thoroughly enjoyed the learning experience and has been able to add "published author" to her resume.

You can follow Ashley on Twitter (@amdchiasson) or find out more about her through her website (http://ashleychiasson.com).

I would first like to thank my husband, Joe, for his support, patience, and tolerance of my long-standing habit of procrastinating. Secondly, I would like to thank my parents for not pressuring me to become an over-achiever in my youth and for always supporting me. Without my editors, this book would have never gotten finished, and without the foreword of Amy Poehler's *Yes Please*, *Dey Street Books*, this book would have taken a lot longer to write. Finally, I want to thank Articulate for building such an awesome product and for letting me make it my muse, and the Articulate E-Learning Heroes Community for helping me grow as an e-learning professional.

About the Reviewers

Asma Shaikh is a human capital consultant with a keen interest in e-learning tools and technology. She has 7 years of experience, the majority of which is in learning and development. She has worked on various e-learning tools and is passionate about creating a new form of learning to capture user attention with minimalistic efforts.

Farhaan Shaikh graduated with a degree in computer engineering from the University of Mumbai. His final year project, a standalone learning environment that made course materials available for anyone connected on a local network, piqued his interests in using technology to train people using a combination of online tutorials and assessments.

He is currently working with a leading provider of corporate training solutions that helps its clients to identify training needs for their employees and develops learning solutions that can be deployed on client workstations to train its workforce.

Although *Articulate Storyline Essentials* is the first book on which Farhaan has worked as a technical reviewer, his journey with Packt Publishing goes far back. He has worked as a technical editor for Packt Publishing and has helped with the production of two other books—*Microsoft System Center 2012 Configuration Manager: Administration Cookbook* and *Piwik Web Analytics Essentials*.

> I would like to thank my colleagues who were very understanding, helpful, and flexible about the timely delivery of my work, as my time was split between commitments at work and meeting the tight production schedules of this book. Also, it was fun to bounce around ideas about the kind of topics that can and cannot go into a book such as this, which aims to give a broad overview of the kind of functionalities that a developer might expect to be available when creating learning courses using Storyline.

Amit Kumar Soni is a dynamic professional with over 6 years of experience in instructional design and e-learning training delivery. He has remarkable experience in producing graphics and animation to support e-learning, training material, and design content. He is a creative guy, proficient with graphics tools (Adobe Photoshop and Illustrator) and authoring tools (Storyline and Captivate) to develop interactive multimedia learning courses.

Currently, he is working with an American MNC, who works with cloud technology (Salesforce, Workday, and Cornerstone). Previously, he was working with an Indian MNC, Larsen & Toubro, as an assistant manager. He received outstanding feedback during his one-year onsite experience working with a Japanese company in Yokohama, Japan.

He is a Microsoft Certified Professional and also holds a certification in Advance Instructional Design from Symbiosis, Pune. He received his bachelor's of engineering in computer science in 2008 and postgraduate diploma in marketing/HR in 2011. He has also been the recipient of the Innovative Trainer Award, 2013, from ISTD, Vadodara, India.

He is a web geek, performing all activities using the resources available on the Internet. He loves to learn new technology and skills. He has his own personal website for writing blogs on social networking sites. In addition to blogging, he enjoys taking photos and reading self-help books as a hobby. He is also a part of an NGO, SGI (Japan). He currently resides in Jaipur, India, with his wonderful wife, Deepty Verma. You can reach him on his website, `amitksoni.com`.

Helen Tyson is an experienced trainer of instructional designer and e-learning developer. She has been involved in training for over 15 years, focusing specifically on e-learning since 2006. She has worked in a variety of industries, including telecommunications, e-mail order retail, financial services, and clinical software production.

After using several other content development software packages, Helen found Articulate Studio in 2009 and has not looked back since then. This led her to take part in the very first Articulate Certified Training course held in the UK for Articulate Studio.

Currently, Helen is an e-learning consultant and the lead trainer for Omniplex Ltd., a company that provides a comprehensive range of e-learning solutions to customers across the UK, Europe, North America, and Asia. Omniplex is the only Articulate Certified Training Partner in the UK and Ireland, and a large part of Helen's role is to deliver the Articulate Certified Program for Storyline, Studio, and Instructional Design.

In addition to training, she also manages a team of trainers, works on content development projects, course consultancy, and implements LMS portals. She has previously reviewed *Learning Articulate Storyline, Packt Publishing,* by Stephanie Harnett.

www.PacktPub.com

Support files, eBooks, discount offers, and more

For support files and downloads related to your book, please visit www.PacktPub.com.

Did you know that Packt offers eBook versions of every book published, with PDF and ePub files available? You can upgrade to the eBook version at www.PacktPub.com and as a print book customer, you are entitled to a discount on the eBook copy. Get in touch with us at service@packtpub.com for more details.

At www.PacktPub.com, you can also read a collection of free technical articles, sign up for a range of free newsletters and receive exclusive discounts and offers on Packt books and eBooks.

https://www2.packtpub.com/books/subscription/packtlib

Do you need instant solutions to your IT questions? PacktLib is Packt's online digital book library. Here, you can search, access, and read Packt's entire library of books.

Why subscribe?
- Fully searchable across every book published by Packt
- Copy and paste, print, and bookmark content
- On demand and accessible via a web browser

Free access for Packt account holders

If you have an account with Packt at www.PacktPub.com, you can use this to access PacktLib today and view 9 entirely free books. Simply use your login credentials for immediate access.

Table of Contents

Preface

Have you ever wondered how e-learning developers create such powerfully effective and creative learning solutions? With Articulate Storyline, you don't need to wonder anymore. Storyline is a powerful authoring tool that allows you to take your creativity to the next level and easily author your own stories. It is an e-learning authoring tool that allows you to leverage built-in development functions to quickly create interactive and engaging learning experiences.

What this book covers

Chapter 1, Building Your Story, familiarizes you with the Storyline interface and teaches you how to add new scenes and slides to begin your storytelling journey.

Chapter 2, Using Content to Tell Your Story, explains how you can easily use text, images, and characters to tell your story.

Chapter 3, Using Content to Enhance Your Story, teaches you simple ways of taking your storytelling abilities to the next level by adding small amounts of interactivity throughout your story.

Chapter 4, Making Your Story Come to Life, provides you with a basis for growing your knowledge of triggers, states, and hotspot interactions to create an engaging story.

Chapter 5, Making Your Story More Realistic, explains how you can create a more realistic story through the use of audio and video features.

Chapter 6, Testing Your Learners, identifies basic assessment concepts and explains how you can easily test your learners using Storyline's built-in assessment features.

Chapter 7, Sharing Your Story, teaches you how to create a customized learning experience by modifying the Storyline default player and explains publishing options available to share your story.

What you need for this book

To ensure you reach your full potential in following along with this book, it is recommended to have:

- An Articulate Storyline 1 or Articulate Storyline 2 license or trial
- Any amount of creativity you can muster.

Refer to Articulate's website for a full list of hardware requirements recommended for operating Articulate Storyline.

Who this book is for

This book is intended for anyone and everyone interested in working within Articulate Storyline to develop engaging and practical e-learning projects. From novice users to experienced users wanting to brush up on the basics, this book lets you learn how to easily navigate Storyline to build and publish your very own story.

Conventions

In this book, you will find a number of text styles that distinguish between different kinds of information. Here are some examples of these styles and an explanation of their meaning.

Code words in text, database table names, folder names, filenames, file extensions, pathnames, dummy URLs, user input, and Twitter handles are shown as follows: "This option allows you to import a previously developed Storyline project template (`.storytemplate`)."

New terms and **important words** are shown in bold. Words that you see on the screen, for example, in menus or dialog boxes, appear in the text like this: "To add a new scene, select the **New Scene (1)** icon from the **Home** tab."

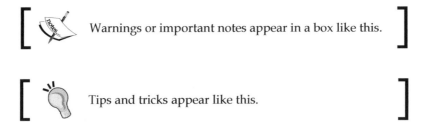

Reader feedback

Feedback from our readers is always welcome. Let us know what you think about this book—what you liked or disliked. Reader feedback is important for us as it helps us develop titles that you will really get the most out of.

To send us general feedback, simply e-mail `feedback@packtpub.com`, and mention the book's title in the subject of your message.

If there is a topic that you have expertise in and you are interested in either writing or contributing to a book, see our author guide at `www.packtpub.com/authors`.

Customer support

Now that you are the proud owner of a Packt book, we have a number of things to help you to get the most from your purchase.

Downloading the color images of this book

We also provide you with a PDF file that has color images of the screenshots/diagrams used in this book. The color images will help you better understand the changes in the output. You can download this file from `https://www.packtpub.com/sites/default/files/downloads/2079OT_ColorImages.pdf`.

Errata

Although we have taken every care to ensure the accuracy of our content, mistakes do happen. If you find a mistake in one of our books—maybe a mistake in the text or the code—we would be grateful if you could report this to us. By doing so, you can save other readers from frustration and help us improve subsequent versions of this book. If you find any errata, please report them by visiting `http://www.packtpub.com/submit-errata`, selecting your book, clicking on the Errata Submission Form link, and entering the details of your errata. Once your errata are verified, your submission will be accepted and the errata will be uploaded to our website or added to any list of existing errata under the Errata section of that title.

To view the previously submitted errata, go to `https://www.packtpub.com/books/content/support` and enter the name of the book in the search field. The required information will appear under the Errata section.

Piracy

Piracy of copyrighted material on the Internet is an ongoing problem across all media. At Packt, we take the protection of our copyright and licenses very seriously. If you come across any illegal copies of our works in any form on the Internet, please provide us with the location address or website name immediately so that we can pursue a remedy.

Please contact us at copyright@packtpub.com with a link to the suspected pirated material.

We appreciate your help in protecting our authors and our ability to bring you valuable content.

Questions

If you have a problem with any aspect of this book, you can contact us at questions@packtpub.com, and we will do our best to address the problem.

1
Building Your Story

Let's get you up and running with Storyline! This chapter provides all you need to know about getting started with your e-learning project.

In this chapter, we will discuss the following topics:

- Introducing Articulate Storyline 2
- Getting started with Articulate Storyline
- Navigating the Storyline interface
- Adding new scenes and slides
- Working from templates
- Importing content
- Saving your story file

Introducing Articulate Storyline 2

Alright! You've installed Articulate Storyline 2, and you are either testing out the trial version or you're interested in using Storyline and want to find out how easy (or hard) it's going to be. Don't fear; I'll make things super easy for you! I can assure you that Storyline is a powerful tool that will likely address all of your e-learning development needs.

So, what is Storyline? Storyline is an authoring tool that allows you to challenge your creativity to produce high-quality, interactive e-learning in a very easy manner! With a user-friendly interface and an incredibly active online community, you can create just about anything your imagination drums up (or reach out to the community if you run into a Storyline situation you're not quite sure how to handle). Having worked with many other authoring tools, I can confidently say that Articulate Storyline is one of my favorite products to author e-learning projects, largely because it is the easiest and most efficient tool I've used, so I think it will quickly become your favorite tool too!

There are some primary differences between Storyline 1 and Storyline 2, which are mentioned here:

- New, flat interface
- Enhanced text editing
- Dockable panels
- Toggling between slide and form views
- Autorecovery
- Slider interactions
- Animation painter
- Motion paths
- Question importing

If you've been working in Storyline 1, you should definitely check out Storyline 2 by downloading the trial version; you can run both programs independently, so you don't need to choose between one or the other. The trial will put you in the driver's seat and allow you enough time (30 days) to try out the new features, in an effort to help you determine whether Storyline 2 is right for you!

Getting started with Articulate Storyline

Whenever you open Storyline 2, you're presented with a start screen. This screen provides you with access to tutorials and downloads, in addition to providing options to create new projects and open recent projects.

 When you're feeling stumped on the way ahead for your project, keep the tutorials and free download options on the start screen in mind; they will likely provide a solution or help you along by providing inspiration. The start screens for both Storyline 1 and Storyline 2 include links to helpful tutorials and free templates/graphics that can be used by course developers.

The following screenshot shows the start screen:

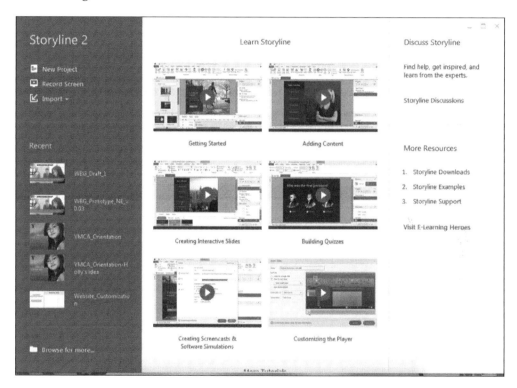

Your options to create a new project include the following:

- **New Project**: This option allows you to start with a blank canvas and autopopulates a starting scene and blank slide.

- **Record Screen**: This option allows you to record screen content and integrate it into a new story.

- **Import**: When you select this option, you will be provided with the following five options:

    ° **Import PowerPoint**: This option allows you to import content or templates previously developed in Microsoft PowerPoint.

    ° **Import Quizmaker**: This option allows you to import content previously developed in Articulate Quizmaker.

    ° **Import Engage**: This option allows you to import content previously developed in Articulate Engage.

    ° **Import questions from file:** This option is only available in Storyline 2 and allows you to import questions from text files (.txt) or Microsoft Excel. Importing questions from files will be discussed in *Chapter 6, Testing Your Learners*.

    ° **Import from Storyline template**: This option allows you to import a previously developed Storyline project template (.storytemplate). You can also use this option to import Storyline content saved with a .story extension.

 To import Articulate Engage or Articulate Storyline content in Storyline 1, you will need to select **File** (the Articulate logo), **Import**, and either the **Engage** option or Storyline icon, depending on the content you wish to import.

Storyline gives you tons of options to start your project, so determine the best option for your needs and make your selection to get started!

Story View is one of my favorite features of Storyline. It provides an overall view of your project, making it extremely easy to organize your scenes and slides, and I like to use it to chunk my project in a logical manner. Alternatively, **Story View** can be a great way to create a visual guide for your project template, allowing your colleagues or clients to see what each screen style will look like—it is great for prototyping!

Story View also allows you to easily see the flow of your project by illustrating triggers (using lines and arrows), which, when hovered over, will reveal the assigned trigger or path. From **Story View**, you can easily see which slides or scenes are branching to other slides or scenes, and it helps streamline the overall development by taking the guesswork out of structuring your course.

 The easiest way to switch to Slide View is to double-click on a slide; however, you can also select the **Slide View** button. In Storyline 2, you can quickly toggle back to Story View by selecting the **Story View** tab when you are in Slide View.

The following screenshot shows the buttons to toggle between different views:

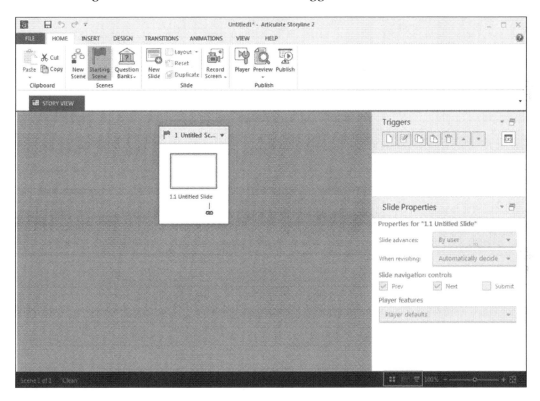

The Storyline interface predominantly uses ribbons and tabs to access various functions, similar to PowerPoint. Each tab opens up a ribbon that contains the options within that tab. You also have a quick access toolbar (**1**) and a **File** button (**2**), which is indicated by the Articulate logo:

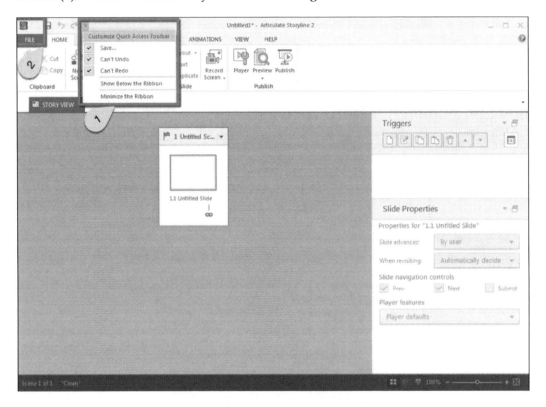

Adding new scenes and slides

Adding new scenes and slides is very easy. To add a new scene, select the **New Scene** (1) icon from the **Home** tab.

>
> When adding a new scene, consider whether you need to move your starting scene (the first scene that will display in your course). To do this, select the scene that you want as the starting scene and select the **Starting Scene** (2) icon from the **Home** tab.

To add a new slide, simply select the **New Slide** (3) icon from the **Home** tab in either Story or Slide View. When in **Story View**, make sure you first select the scene in which you want to add the new slide.

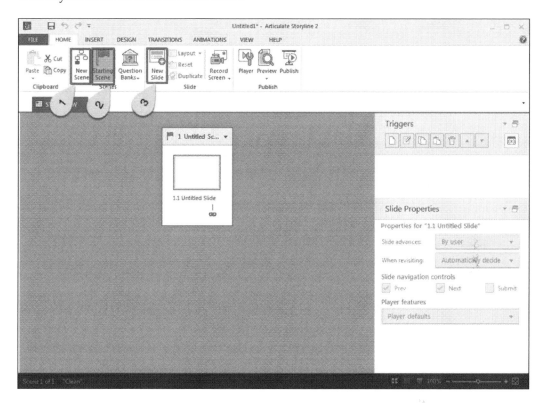

Working from a template

Now, I'm probably not going to be the first to tell you that if there's a way of making your life easier, occasionally, you should take the opportunity presented. Templates are one of those opportunities! Templates can make your day that much better when you're working on a large project that needs a little streamlining. The built-in templates within Storyline can also be a great starting point for inspiration; they're easily modifiable, and with all of the free downloads kicking around, you can really leverage your project design with minimal effort.

There are a few ways you can work from a Storyline template; they are as follows:

- You can double-click on a Storyline template file saved to your computer
- You can open Storyline and click on Import (process discussed in the next section)
- You can navigate to **File | Import | Storyline**, or you can select **New Slide** and select a slide from the **Templates** tab:

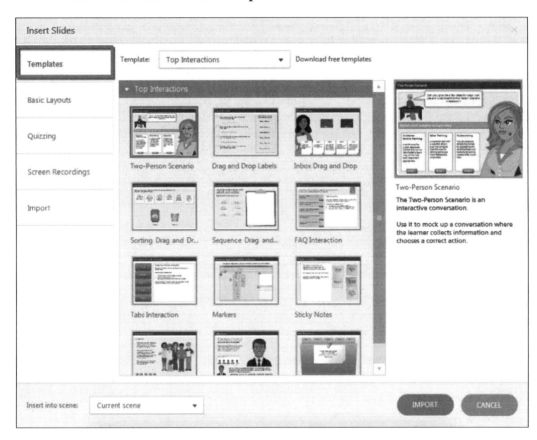

Importing content

On the start screen, there are five options to import content: **Import PowerPoint**, **Import Quizmaker**, **Import Engage**, **Import from story template**, and **Import questions from file**.

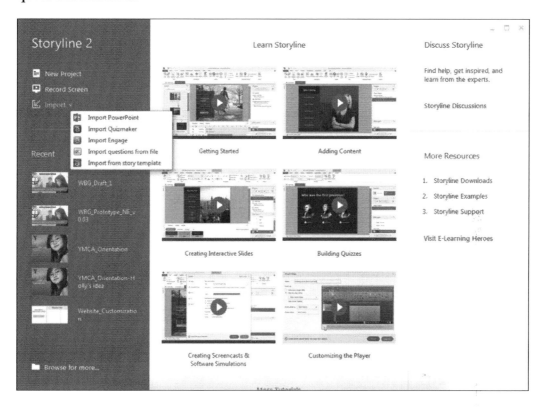

Importing from PowerPoint

To import content from PowerPoint, select **Import PowerPoint**, browse for
the PowerPoint file you wish to import, and select **Import**. You will be presented
with a series of slides (those contained within the selected PowerPoint file), and
you can either import all of them or select those you wish to import. From the
drop-down menu, choose which scene you want to import the slides to and then
select the **IMPORT** button. All the selected PowerPoint slides will then be imported
into the scene you specified.

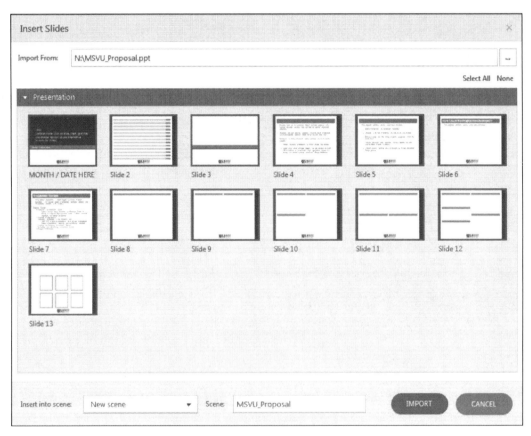

Importing from Quizmaker

To import content from Quizmaker, select **Import Quizmaker**, browse for the `.quiz` file you wish to import, and select **Import**. You will be presented with a series of slides (those contained within the selected Quizmaker file), and you can either import all or select those you wish to import. From the drop-down menu, choose which scene you want to import the slides to and then select the **IMPORT** button. All the selected Quizmaker slides will then be imported into the scene you specified.

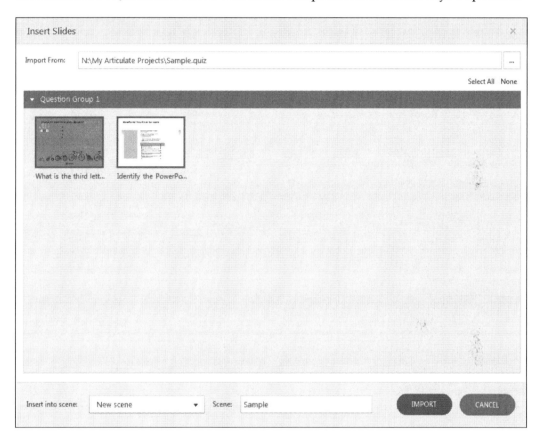

Importing from Storyline

To import content from Storyline, select **Import from story template**, browse for the story file you wish to import, and select **Import**. You will be presented with a series of slides (those contained within the selected Storyline file), and you can either import all or select those you wish to import. From the drop-down menu, choose which scene you want to import the slides to, and then select the **IMPORT** button. All selected Storyline slides will then be imported into the scene you specified.

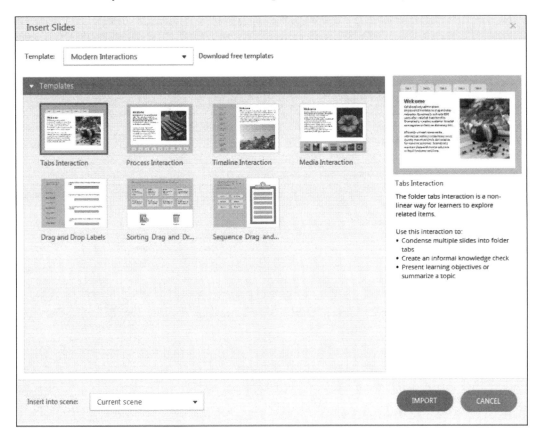

Importing from Articulate Engage

To import content from Articulate Engage, select **Import Engage**, browse for the Engage file you wish to import, and select **Import**. You will be presented with the Engage interactions contained within the Engage file, and you can either import all of them or select those you wish to import. From the drop-down menu, choose which scene you want to import the slides to and then select the **IMPORT** button. All the selected Engage interactions will then be imported into the scene you specified.

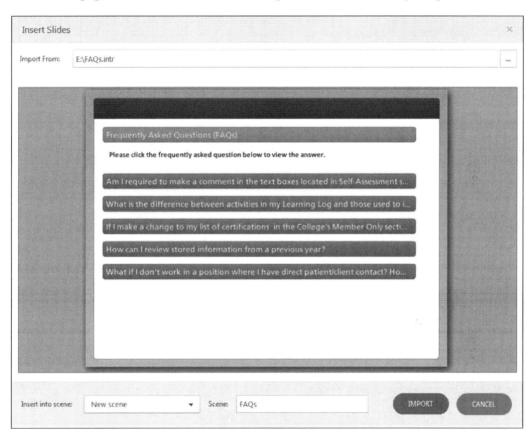

Once the content has been imported, you will be able to edit these slides fully within Storyline.

Saving your story

Saving your story is a critical factor—trust me, you don't want to spend hours (or days) on a project without saving it, only to have Storyline crash when you're publishing... or sooner. Storyline 2 has an autosave feature; however, Storyline 1 does not, and you really don't want to be nearing the end of a critical deadline having to replicate the last 30 hours of work. We've all been there, and it's an awful feeling.

The moral of this story is save your story, and save it often!

To save your story, you can use the keyboard shortcut *Ctrl + S*, or you can navigate to the **File** tab and select either **Save** or **Save As**:

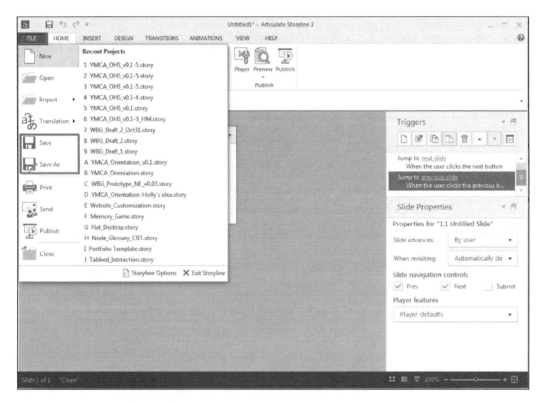

Summary

This chapter introduced you to Articulate Storyline 2, some of the main differences between Storyline 1 and Storyline 2, and some key concepts to get started with a new project in Storyline. You should now be able to easily create a new project using blank scenes and slides; create a project from a template; or import content from PowerPoint, Articulate Engage, or Articulate Quizmaker to create a new project.

Now that you have the basics out of the way, you should be ready to get started and let your storytelling abilities grow! In the next chapter, I will show you how to use content to tell your story. You'll discover how to add and format text, insert images, and add characters—it might seem basic, but these elements will be critical to effectively telling your story!

2
Using Content to Tell Your Story

Now that you are up and running with Storyline, we're going to discuss some of the basic functions that are important for sharing your story. This chapter explains how to insert text, images, and characters to enhance your storytelling abilities!

In this chapter, we will be discussing the following topics:

- Telling your story
- Adding and formatting text
- Inserting images
- Adding characters

Telling your story

When you develop e-learning projects, you're essentially telling a story. It might be the story of how to remove or install the rotor blades of an aircraft, or it might be a story about how to prevent workplace violence. Whatever story you're going to tell, Storyline has a variety of content options that will facilitate your storytelling.

Adding and formatting text

Adding text is essential to any course; I am yet to see one that doesn't make use of text…don't quote me on that.

To add text, you will need to access the **Insert** tab and then select **Text Box** as shown in the following screenshot:

 Alternatively, you can use the shortcut key combination *Ctrl + T*, and a textbox will magically appear on your slide.

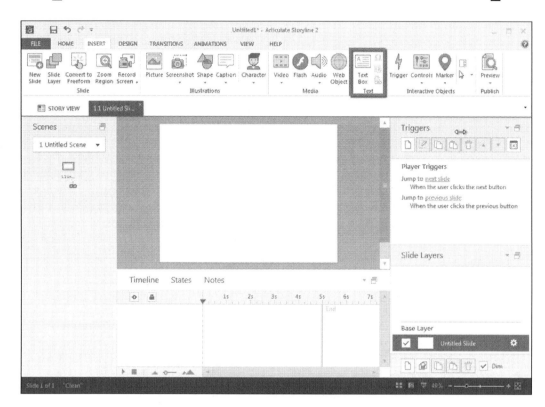

Once you have added some text to your screen, you can select the text to format it. You have several options for formatting, and I'll provide you with a brief summary of these options:

- **Option 1**: From the **Home** tab, you can highlight your text and adjust the size, the appearance (bold/italics/underlined) of the text itself, or your can adjust the appearance of the textbox by applying an outline or fill. In the **Paragraph** section, you can adjust line spacing, whether your text is bulleted, the direction of the text, and the text alignment as shown in the following screenshot.

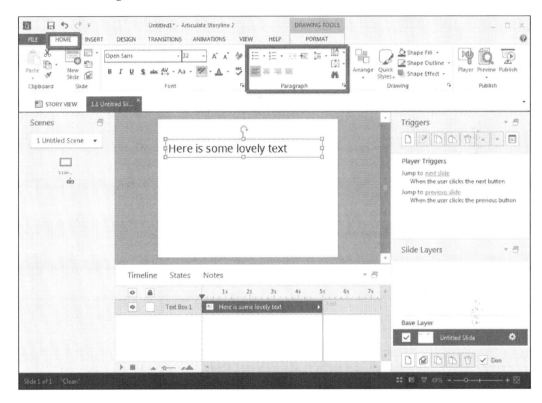

- **Option 2**: With the textbox selected, you can also format your text using the **Format** tab as highlighted in the following screenshot. Here, you have several of the same options as you do on the **Home** tab; however, these are almost exclusively related to the textbox itself, and not the text. Here, you can apply an outline or fill, rotate, or add an effect to the textbox—and much more. While formatting from the **Format** tab can be handy, it's not as practical as formatting from the **Home** tab. The **Home** tab provides you with more text-editing-specific options, and as a best practice, I would recommend formatting from this tab.

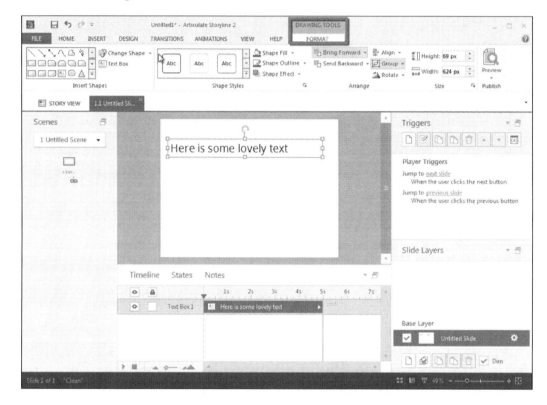

- **Option 3**: If you're like me, you probably like to get down to the nuts and bolts of things when it comes to formatting. In that case, **Option 3** will be your new best pal! Here you will format your text using the **Format Shape** option. To access this, select your text, right-click, and select **Format Shape** as shown in the following screenshot:

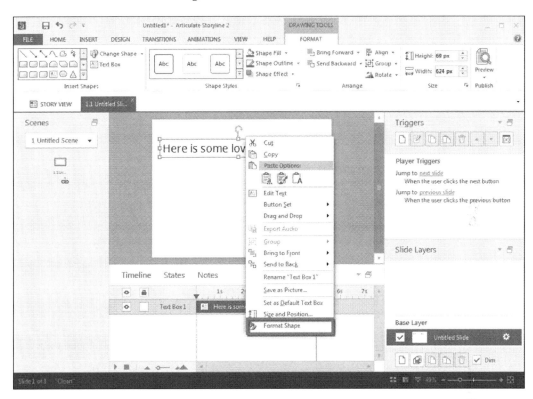

You will be presented with a **Format Shape** menu as shown in the following screenshot, and you will want to select the **Text Box** tab. Here, you will be able to tinker with the vertical alignment, auto fit, and internal margins. Once you have finished tinkering, you can select **CLOSE** to view the now formatted text on your screen.

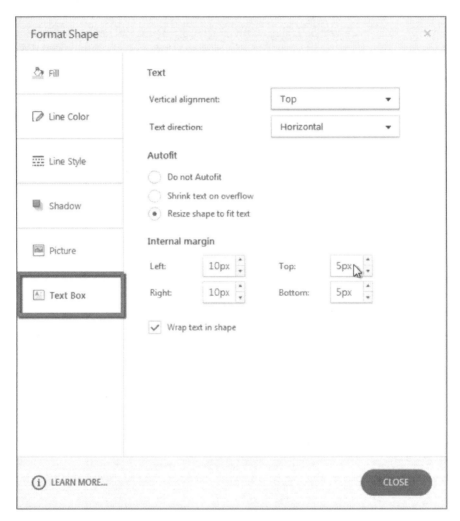

Inserting images

There are two types of images you can add to your story: pictures and screenshots as shown in the following screenshot.

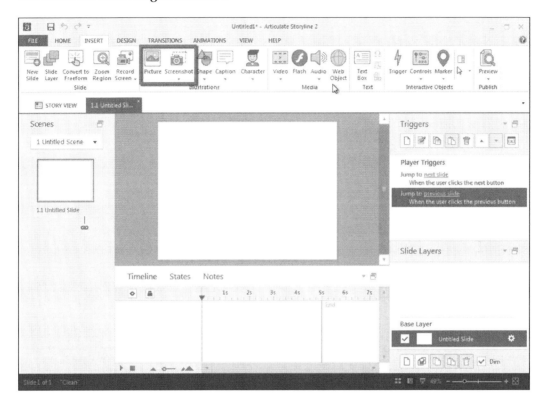

Inserting a picture is pretty simple; you just select the **Picture** icon from the **Insert** ribbon, browse for the picture, and then double-click.

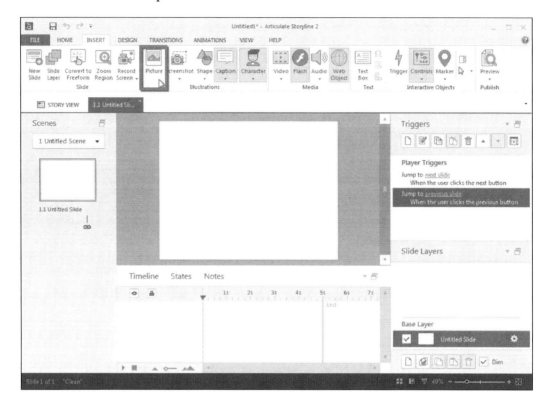

Once added, you can easily format the picture by either selecting the **Format** tab (**1**) or by right-clicking and selecting **Format Picture** (**2**).

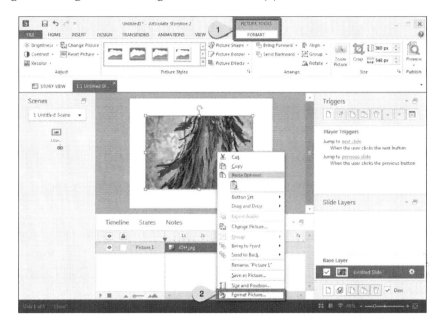

Formatting allows you to recolor, use presets, and adjust variables such as brightness, contrast, and transparency. You can also rotate, zoom in on, or crop the picture.

Using the formatting features is an easy way to customize graphics without knowing anything about graphic design. The options provided allow you to adjust the image to your liking and to suit the needs of your course.

Another cool feature in Storyline is that once you have an image in place, you can easily replace the picture and maintain most of the formatting (depending on the size of the image, the overall size may differ) by right-clicking on the picture and selecting **Change Picture** as shown in the following screenshot.

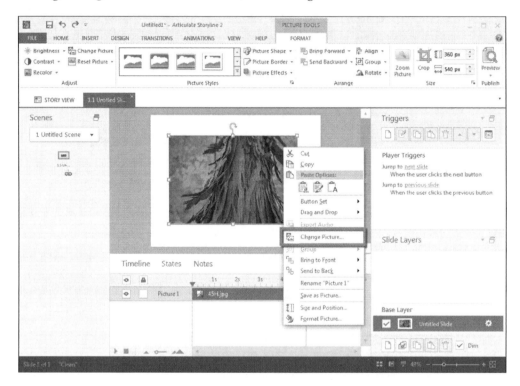

Inserting screenshots

Screenshots allow you to capture a portion of your computer screen as an image. To insert a screenshot, select the **Screenshot** icon in the **Insert** tab, and then select **Screen Clipping**:

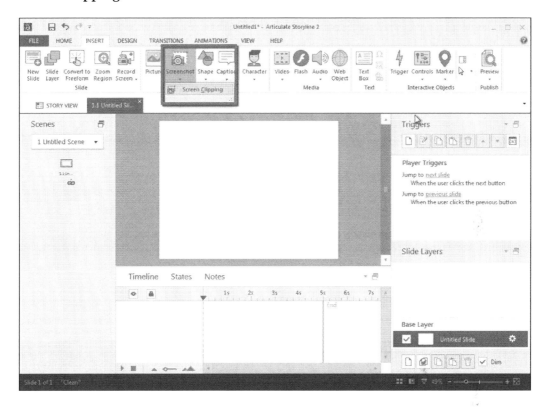

Once selected, you will be able to select the area of your computer screen that you would like to capture as shown in the following screenshot, and select it using the crosshair icon. Your selection will then be imported into your Storyline screen, and you are able to format the screenshot as you would a picture.

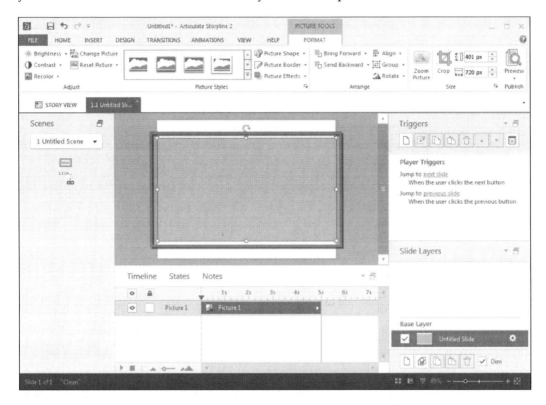

Adding characters

Characters can be used to bring life to your course and provide a realistic element. You have two options when adding characters: **Illustrated Character** or **Photographic Character**.

Storyline is equipped with several default illustrated and photographic characters, both containing a series of available poses. However, the illustrated characters tend to have more flexibility in their pose and expression range.

To add an illustrated character, select **Character** from the **Insert** tab (**1**), and then select **Illustrated Character** (**2**):

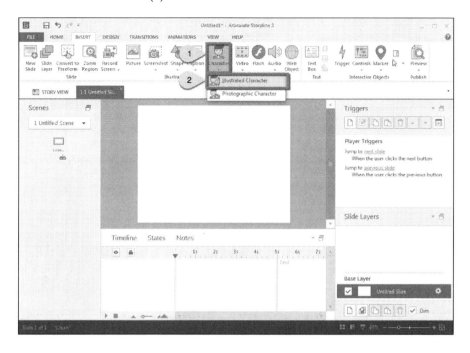

A character menu will appear, and you will need to first select your **Character** (**1**), and whether you want them to be posed **Left**, **Front**, or **Right** (**2**):

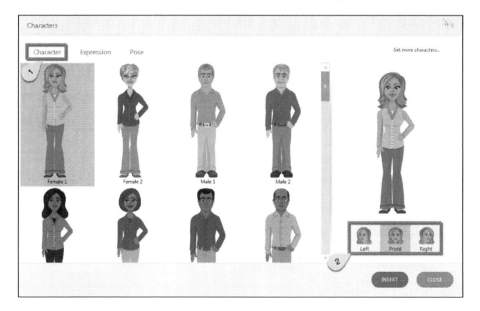

Once you have selected your character and their position, you can then select their **Expression** or **Pose** by selecting the appropriate term at the top of the character menu.

Expressions can help your character convey emotions relative to the material you are presenting. For example, if your screen content relates to the concept of workplace stress, you can choose to have your character appear stressed:

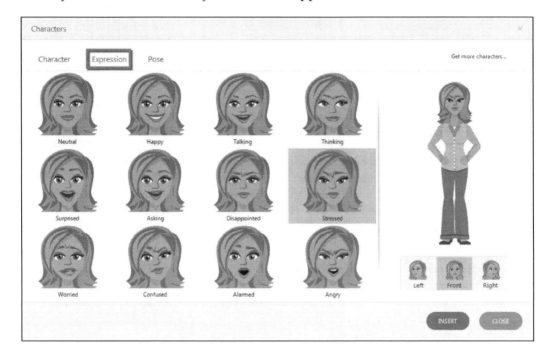

Adjusting the pose of your character can help orient the learner to the context of the material being discussed. In the example of workplace stress, our character may work within an inbound call center environment, and is perhaps dealing with an irate customer. To contextualize this scenario for your learners, you can choose to place the character in a context-based pose, sitting at a desk and talking on the phone:

Once you have selected your character, their expression, and their pose, you can select **Insert**, and your character will be added to your slide as shown in the following screenshot.

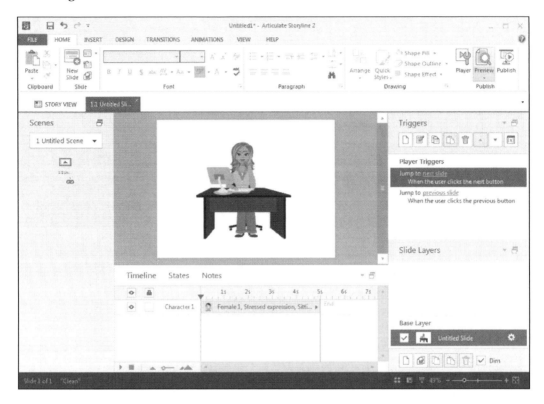

As your characters are vector-based images, they can be scaled however large you like. You can also format your character using the **Character Tools** tab as highlighted in the following screenshot. Here, you can change the character, expression, or pose. Additionally, you will be able to format your character in the same manner as if you were formatting a picture.

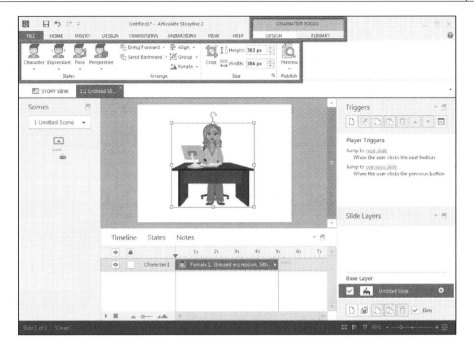

To insert a photographic character, select **Character** from the **Insert** tab (**1**), and then select **Photographic Character** (**2**):

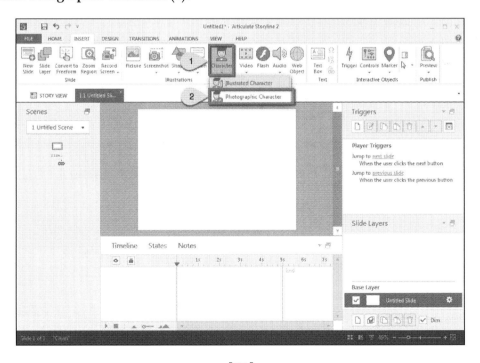

Similar to the **Illustrated Character** option, you will be provided with some character options—these are the most realistic ones as they are real-life human beings, rather than illustrations. Once you have selected your character (**1**), you can choose how much of your character you would like to display: **Headshot**, **Torso**, or **Full** (**2**):

Once you have decided on a character and how much of them you would like to display, you can choose their pose. As with the illustrated characters, the pose can provide context for your learners, so you should ensure you are selecting a relevant pose for the onscreen content. In this example, I want to convey that the user has answered a quiz question incorrectly, so I am using an *oops* pose for my character:

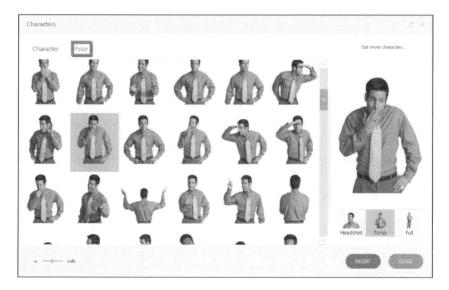

Once you have determined your character, display orientation, and pose, you can select **Insert**, and your character will be inserted onto your screen. As with the illustrated character, the photographic characters are fully scalable, and you can format them using the **Character Tools** tab as shown in the following screenshot.

Summary

This chapter provided you with several options to tell your story: through text, using images, and using characters. Your ability to become a storyteller savant can easily be supported by Storyline, and you should now have a solid understanding of how to easily incorporate and format text, pictures, and characters.

In the next chapter, I will show you how to use content to enhance your story. You'll discover how to add and format buttons, markers, and hyperlinks. These elements can be viewed as building blocks to incorporating more robust interactivity within your courses, which will be discussed further in *Chapter 4, Making Your Story Come to Life*.

3
Using Content to Enhance Your Story

Now that you've learned how to insert and format text, pictures, and characters, you should be prepared to learn about some additional Storyline features that can enhance your story. This chapter explains how to inject small doses of interactivity by adding and editing buttons, markers, and hyperlinks.

In this chapter, we will discuss the following topics:

- Easy ways to enhance your story
- Adding and formatting buttons
- Adding and formatting markers
- Inserting hyperlinks

Easy ways to enhance your story

Buttons, markers, and hyperlinks are all options that allow you to easily enhance your story, allowing you to add interactivity with minimal effort. These interactive objects will provide you with options to customize the look and feel of your story, and I'll explain how these functions can inadvertently maximize your screen real estate.

Adding and formatting buttons

Buttons are an easy way of creating functional activity within any course. You can use them to create custom next and previous buttons, or you can use them to trigger other events (for example, moving to the next scene or changing the state of an element on screen, just to name a couple of functions). Buttons are one of the most usable features within Storyline!

You can add buttons in one of two ways:

- Selecting **Controls** on the **Insert** tab
- Creating a **Custom** button, using the `shape` function

We'll explore both of these options further.

Selecting a new button

To add a button, select **Controls** on the **Insert** tab. You will be provided with several options. Storyline comes equipped with two basic buttons, four checkboxes, and four radio buttons, as shown in the following screenshot:

 The **Insert** tab has changed a bit between Storyline 1 and Storyline 2. If you are using Storyline 1, you will find the buttons by going to the **Insert** tab and selecting **Button**.

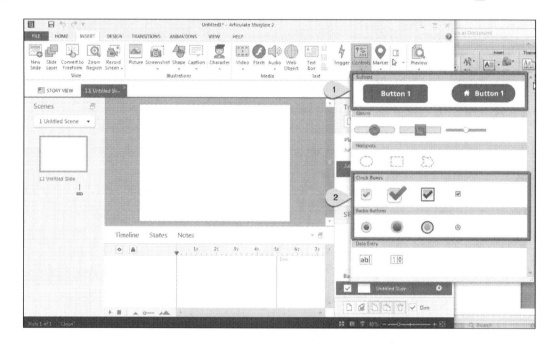

Determine which button style you wish to use and select it. For the purpose of this example, we are using one of the text buttons. Then, you can either left-click on your screen or click and drag to draw the button where you want it to appear on your screen.

You will notice that two things occur: your button is applied to your screen and an empty trigger for your button has appeared in the trigger panel. The trigger will be used to make your button functional; but we'll come back to that a little later on.

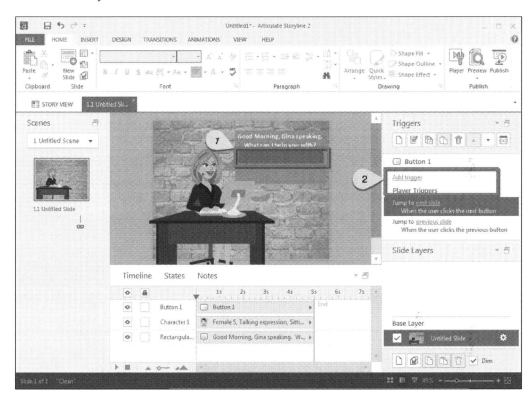

Storyline also has some built-in custom states for the button feature. Whenever you add a button and click on **States**, you will see that there are five states pre-populated. These states provide a little pizzazz to your otherwise static buttons.

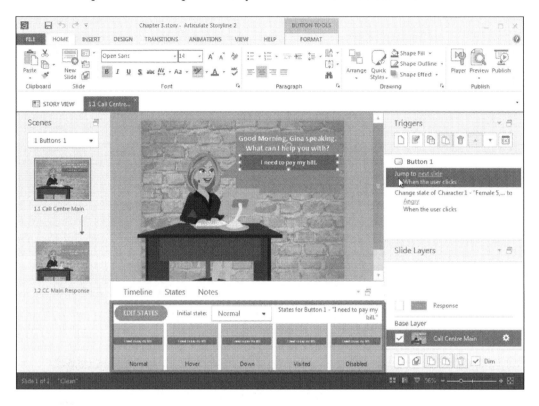

Now, you probably want to add some text to this button to make it meaningful to your users. To do this, you do not need to add an additional textbox; you can simply select your button and type the desired text. The text will default to center alignment within the button. If you're familiar with using Microsoft PowerPoint, you will quickly realize that adding and editing text in Storyline is similar to adding and editing text for shapes in PowerPoint.

 If you're new to Storyline, your gut might tell you to add text to your button by adding a textbox, but resist this urge. It will save you the headache when you realize your triggers aren't working properly later on.

The following screenshot shows how text can be added to a button without creating an additional textbox:

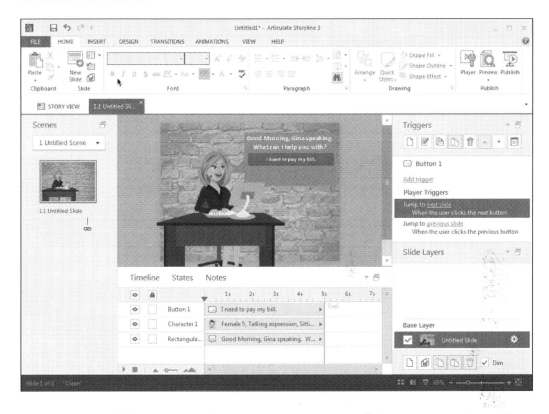

Once you've added text to your button, your next step will be to create a trigger. In this example, we will set the button trigger on the trigger panel to show the response layer. A layer is used to display additional content without requiring an additional screen, or to display content as a response to a user action.

We'll talk more about all the triggers Storyline offers in the following chapter; here, we will discuss one specific example for setting your button trigger: jump to the next slide. First, you will need to select the **Add Trigger** hyperlink in the **Triggers** panel under **Button 1**.

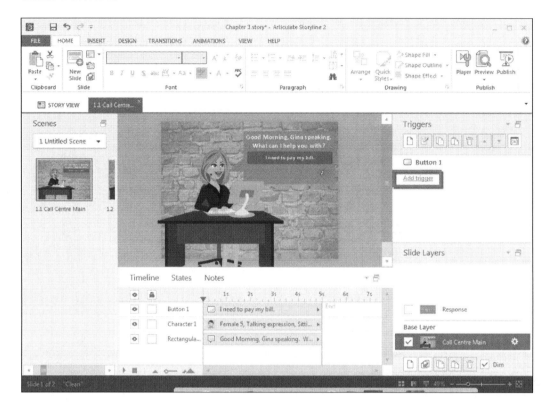

A **Trigger Wizard** dialog box will appear. Within the **Trigger Wizard** dialog box, you will dictate how you want the button to behave. In this example, we want to jump to the next slide when the user clicks on **Button 1**, so we will set up our trigger as follows:

- **Action**: **Jump to slide**
- **Slide**: **Next slide**
- **When**: **User clicks**
- **Object**: **Button 1**

The following screenshot shows the **Trigger Wizard** dialog box:

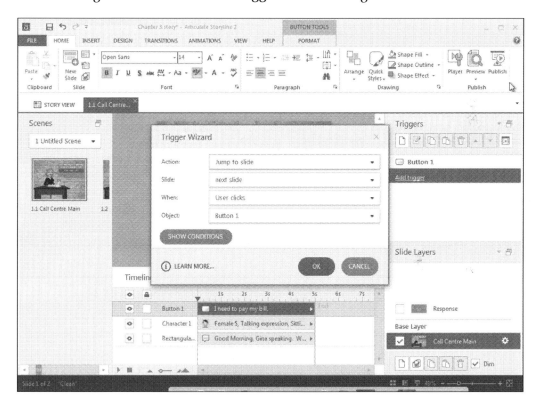

Once you have selected these variables from the appropriate drop-down menus, click on **OK**. You will see that your trigger has been applied to **Button 1**, and that your screen now links to the next slide.

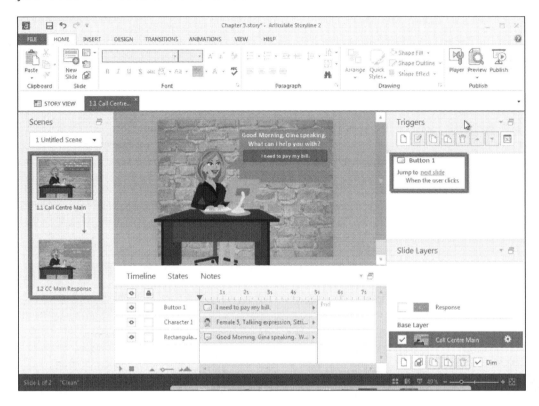

Now that you've made your button *work*, you might want to change the formatting to closely match your design aesthetics. You can easily do this using the **Button Tools Format** tab.

The **Button Tools Format** tab allows you to add icons to the button, adjust the colors and effects, and even adjust the button trigger.

Now, it might seem as though it was long ago, but I did mention that there were two options for adding buttons in *Chapter 2, Using Content to Tell Your Story* .

Creating a new shape

Option 2 is to create a new shape by selecting **Shape** on the **Insert** menu, selecting the desired shape, and clicking on or clicking and dragging it on to the screen to create your shape. Creating a custom shape works similar to using a button; however, a placeholder trigger isn't applied, so you will need to do this manually; you'll learn more about this in *Chapter 4, Making Your Story Come to Life*.

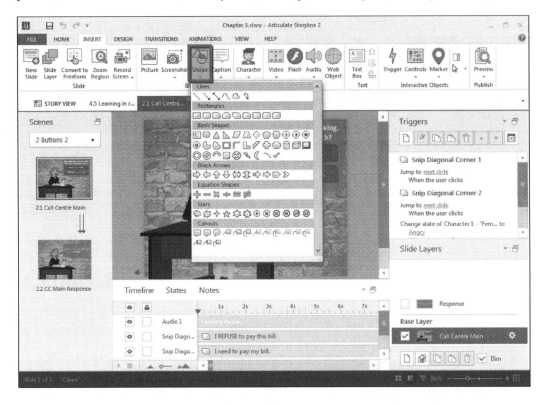

You can format the shape in the same manner you would with the button; however, you will access the formatting options by clicking the shape on your screen and then selecting the **Format** tab.

> Note that you will be unable to modify the trigger from the shape **Format** menu; you will need to do this manually within the **Triggers** panel on the right. Additionally, your shape will not have any custom states autopopulated, so you will need to add these manually if you wish to jazz up your static buttons.

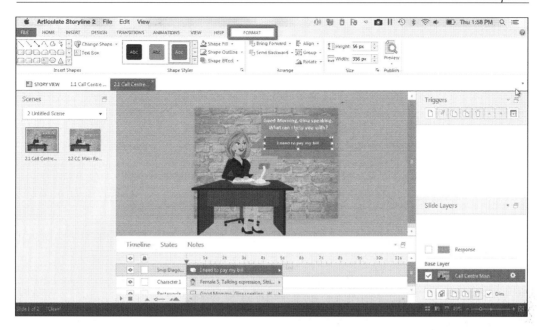

Using markers

Markers are a great way to turn static screens into something a bit more interactive. They also give you the opportunity to expand your screen real estate by containing text you may have otherwise placed on the screen itself.

Instead, your audience will get to see more of the screen content and imagery, while stashing all the good information away—which can either be text-only, audio-only, images, or a combination of any of those elements—in a hover and revealing or clicking and revealing the marker. Sneaky interactivity is the best kind!

One of the most common uses for markers is to display textual content associated with a relevant portion of the screen. For example, if you were looking at a map, markers may be used to display city-related statistics. In this example, I'll be calling attention to the anatomy of a friendly wildlife creature, the bear.

To add a marker, select **Marker** from the **Insert** tab and choose the icon that speaks to your design need. Or, if none of the built-in options work, select the blank marker.

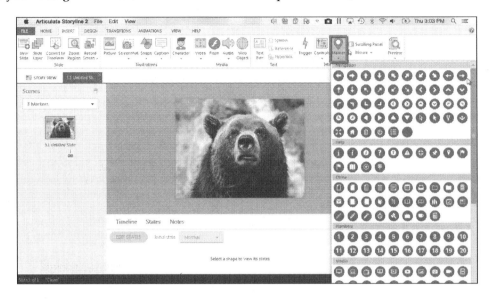

Once you have selected your marker icon, click on your screen. The marker will appear on your screen along with its description box. You can click and drag the marker wherever you would like to place it.

You can format the text for your marker using the text formatting options available on the **Home** tab, and you can customize the look of your marker by using the **Format** tab. Here, you can change the marker icon, colors, and animating effect, to name just a few.

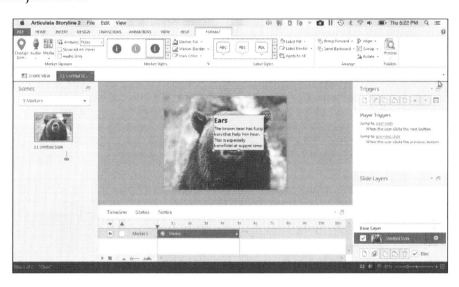

Within the **Format** tab, you can also choose to add audio or other multimedia to your marker, if you feel it is of value. This is a great way to add supporting content. For example, when talking about the bear's ears, we might include a picture of the bear's inner ear anatomy. To add media, simply click on either **Audio** or **Media** within the **Format** tab, and browse for the file you want to insert.

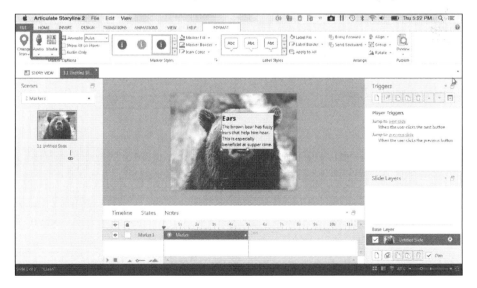

Adding hyperlinks

Hyperlinks allow users to navigate to different sections of the course or to external web pages and/or documents.

To insert a hyperlink, highlight the item on the screen (for example, text, image, and so on) you wish to convert into a link and then navigate to the **Insert** tab and select **Hyperlink**, as shown in the following screenshot:

 To create a hyperlink, you can also highlight the screen item you wish to convert into a link and use the hotkeys *Ctrl + K*.

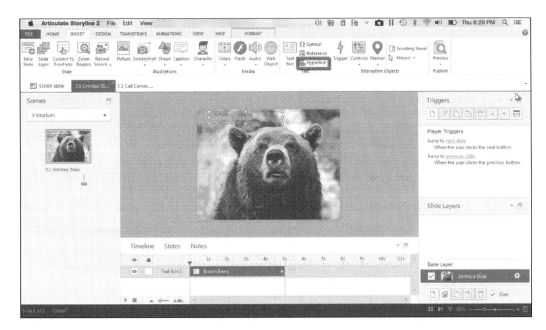

You'll be presented with the **Trigger Wizard**; notice that the **Action** is **Jump to URL/File**. Enter the URL for the website you wish to link to or use the browse option to locate the file you wish to link to, and select **OK**.

If you wish to jump to another scene, slide, or lightbox slide, you can easily do so by changing the **Action** drop-down menu to the appropriate selection. Once selected, you will then navigate to the appropriate scene, slide, or layer, using the drop-down menu that appears below the **Action** menu. (For example, if the **Action** is **Show layer**, the drop-down menu layer will appear below **Action**, but if the **Action** is **Jump to URL/File**, the **File** menu will appear below **Action**.)

The screen item you highlighted will now appear as a hyperlink.

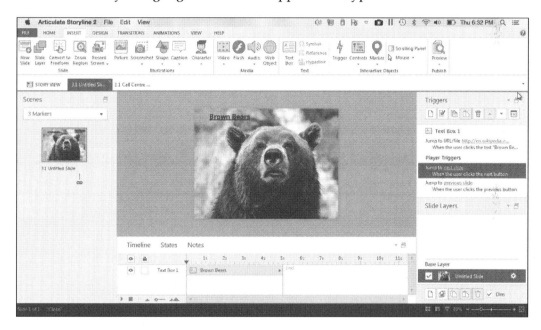

The hyperlink text will default to a blue color, but you can format your hyperlink just as you would format text by highlighting the relevant text and using the text formatting options located on the **Home** tab.

Summary

This chapter provided you with several options for using content to enhance your story: using buttons, markers, and hyperlinks. These Storyline functions allow you to engage your audience with tidbits of interactivity, without having to worry about developing complicated interactions.

Storyline's built-in buttons and markers can easily allow you to transform traditional static elements into animated course components, and the ability to create hyperlinks within your course will provide you with the opportunity to link to internal or external content.

In the next chapter, you will see how to make your story come to life! You'll learn how to use triggers, states, and hotspots. Building on what you've learned in this chapter, these elements will teach you how to engage your audience with interactivity.

4
Making Your Story Come to Life

Now that you've learned some ways to incorporate basic interactivity, you should be ready to build on that knowledge by learning about some more complex ways of creating interactive elements within your story. This chapter explains how to amplify the interactivity in your story by using triggers, states, and hotspots.

In this chapter, we will be discussing the following topics:

- Ways to make your story come to life
- Using triggers
- Using states
- Using hotspots

Ways to make your story come to life

Triggers, **states**, and **hotspots** are all elements that will make your story come to life. These elements will allow you to create enhanced interactivity, and liven up your story with actions. You can use these elements to customize your story and take your learner on an engaging learning experience.

As alluded to in the previous chapter, these elements are essential Storyline functions, and we'll be discussing how you can harness the power of triggers, states, and hotspots to take your static story and transform it into an interactive empire—the only real limit is how far you want to let your creativity take you.

Using triggers

Triggers allow you to create conditional interactivity. They are incredibly versatile, in that, you can add a trigger to most screen objects, controlling that object in a sense. It might be hard to believe, but once you begin working consistently in Storyline you will become a Trigger Wizard, using them here, there, and everywhere. So let's get started; there is quite a bit to cover here!

The **Trigger** panel is located on the far right of your screen as shown in the following screenshot:

 In Storyline 2, you have the ability to dock or undock these panels. So by using the icon in the upper-right corner of the **Trigger** panel, you can move this panel, or any other panel, wherever you prefer.

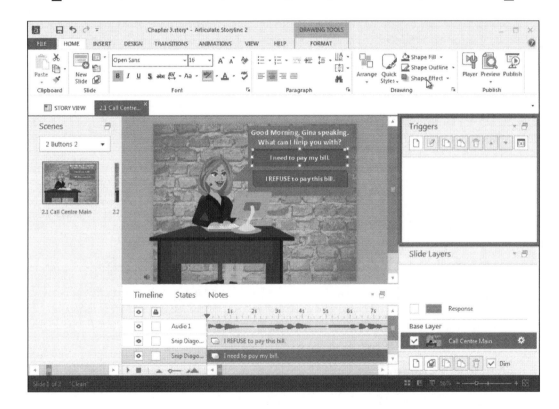

This panel allows you to:

- Create a new trigger
- Edit the selected trigger
- Copy and paste the selected trigger
- Move the trigger up or down in the list of triggers
- Manage your project variables

You will become friends with the **Trigger** panel, and depending on your mood, you might love it or hate it. Regardless of how you feel, you'll need to learn to get along with it—triggers are here to stay!

Talking about triggers is a rabbit hole of excitement and it's easy to get distracted. For the purposes of this book, this section will explain trigger options, with the more common options discussed further. If you want to learn more about triggers, check out *Learning Articulate Storyline* by Stephanie Harnett.

Alright! Let's talk about trigger basics. With triggers, you have options, and loads of them! Storyline separates these options into several groups, and you can easily remember these groups as the *What*, *Where*, and *When*.

The *What* is the action, and this is where you identify the event you want to see happen. In **Trigger Wizard**, this is **Action**.

When you select **Action** from **Trigger Wizard**, you are presented with a drop-down menu containing all of the available actions. These actions are broken down into five types: **Common**, **Media**, **Project**, **More**, and **Quiz**. Here you will select what you want your trigger to do:

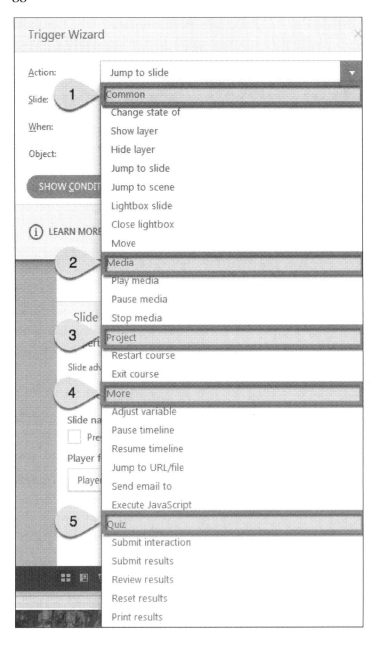

Next, we have the *Where* category. This is where you dictate where you want the action to occur. For example, if I select **Jump to slide**, the next drop-down menu will be categorized as **Slide**. If I select **Show layer**, the next drop-down menu will be categorized as **Layer**. So the menu will change depending on the action you select.

Finally, we have the *When* category. This is where we dictate when the action will occur. Storyline breaks these events into four categories:

- Click Events
- Timeline Events
- Drag Drop Events
- Other Events

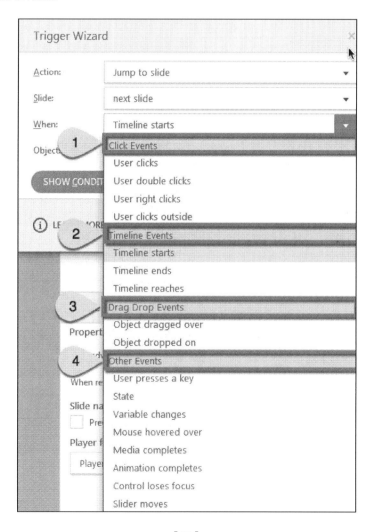

Adding a trigger

So there it is—the basics! You have a lot of options with triggers, and now I'll show you an example of how to make them work. Let's go back to the **Button** example in *Chapter 3, Using Content to Enhance Your Story*. Remember adding a custom shape for a button? Now you will learn two ways of adding a trigger to that shape to turn it into a functional button.

Adding a trigger from the Triggers panel

To create a new trigger, use the following steps:

1. Select the **Create a new trigger** icon on the **Triggers** panel.

2. **Trigger Wizard** will appear, and we will specify our operating parameters. In this example, we want the user to click on the button to move to the next slide, so here is how we do it:

   ° **Action**: **Jump to slide**

   ° **Slide**: **Next slide**

> ○ **When**: User clicks
>
> ○ **Object**: Snip Diagonal Corner 1

3. Once you have set these parameters and have clicked on **OK**, you will see that the two screens have been linked together with the specified action, allowing the user to navigate to the next slide by clicking on the button. You will also notice that there is a trigger in the **Triggers** panel.

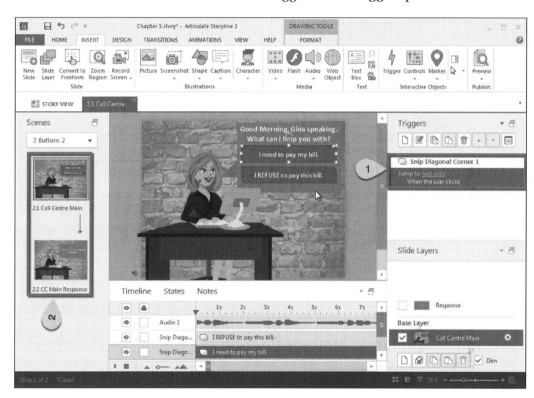

Adding a trigger from the Insert tab

Alternatively, you can add a new trigger by selecting **Trigger** from the **INSERT** tab as shown in the following screenshot, which will call up **Trigger Wizard**. Here, you can specify your operating conditions as discussed in **Option 1** of *Chapter 2, Using Content to Tell Your Story*

If you're using this method, I would recommend selecting the object for which you wish to add a trigger. This will make things easier for you in the long run, especially if your screen consists of many objects. Another important thing to note is that if you copy an object that already has a trigger associated with it, the object's trigger will also be copied; this can help make your development process more efficient.

The best way to learn about how to use triggers is to play around with all of your options, and see what works and what doesn't. Another good analogy for triggers is to think of them similar to that of an if/then statement in Philosophy or computer programming. *If this, then that* — this helps me think clearly about how I want my trigger to behave.

Editing a trigger

It's really easy to edit triggers. All you have to do is select the trigger you wish to edit, and either double-click on the trigger or select the **Edit the selected trigger** icon on the **Triggers** panel, as shown in the following screenshot. Doing either of these things will bring up **Trigger Wizard**, and you can edit your trigger accordingly.

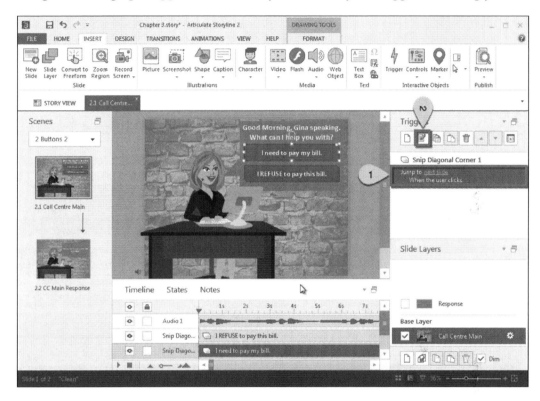

Alternatively, you can also edit a trigger by right-clicking on the trigger in the **Triggers** panel, and select **Edit** from the context menu.

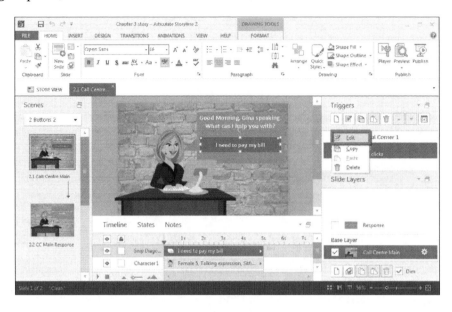

Depending on the trigger type, you may also be able to edit the elements of the trigger without entering **Trigger Wizard**. For example, the **Jump to slide** trigger allows you to select the hyperlinked target slide and change the target location from a drop-down menu of available slides, as shown in the following screenshot:

Deleting a trigger

Deleting a trigger is even easier than editing one! All you need to do is select the relevant trigger, and then select the **Delete the selected trigger** icon from the **Triggers** panel, as shown in the following screenshot. You will be prompted to confirm that you want to delete the selected trigger, and once confirmed, the trigger will be removed. As with editing a trigger, you can also delete a trigger by right-clicking the trigger and selecting **Delete** from the context menu.

Using states

States are an easy way to add interactivity to your story, and they can make otherwise static objects appear more lively. States allow you to change the appearance of static objects based on how the user is interacting with the object. Some of the great ways to use states include:

- Adding effects (for example, shadows or glow) or subtle color changes to buttons or icons
- Displaying additional content
- Creating roll-over style images

The default state for all objects is **Normal**, and you will need to create additional states to objects if you wish to include more than the default state. However, if you insert a button, your button will automatically include five states: **Normal**, **Hover**, **Down**, **Visited**, and **Disabled**. You will also see the **Selected** state if the button is a radio button or checkbox.

To access object states, select an object on your screen and toggle to the **States** panel on **Timeline**, as shown in the following screenshot:

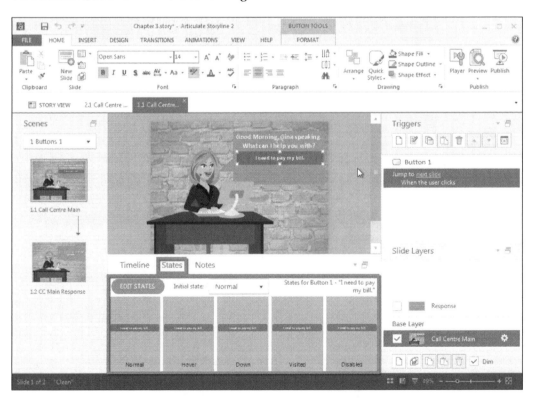

In the preceding example, you can see that the object selected is a button and it comes with five built-in states. As previously mentioned, not all objects come with these built-in states, and instead only have the **Normal** state available, so let's discuss how you can add new states!

Adding a new state

Perhaps we want our call center employee, Gina, to have different facial expressions based on different events. To add a new facial expression to Gina's repertoire, we will need to select **Gina**, toggle to the **States** panel, and click on **EDIT STATES**:

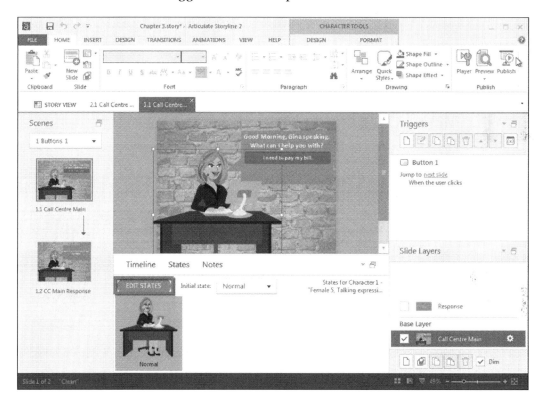

The menu in the **States** panel will change, and to add a new state, you will click on the **New State** icon. An **Add New State** menu will appear; here, you will specify the name of the new state. Once you enter the name, select **Add**:

In this example, I specified **Angry** as the new state, which is an expression that exists within the character repertoire. So when I selected **Add**, the new character state was automatically generated. To exit this menu, click on **Done Editing States**. The following screenshot shows that Gina is angry:

Editing states

Maybe Gina's default expression, **Angry**, isn't quite the angry look you were going for. You can edit her expression by accessing the **States** panel and selecting **Edit States**. Select the state you wish to edit, and from the **Design** tab within **Character Tools**, select **Expression** and identify the expression you would prefer to use for the **Angry** state. Once selected, the new expression will be applied to the state you chose to edit, and you can select **Done Editing States** to exit the **Edit States** menu.

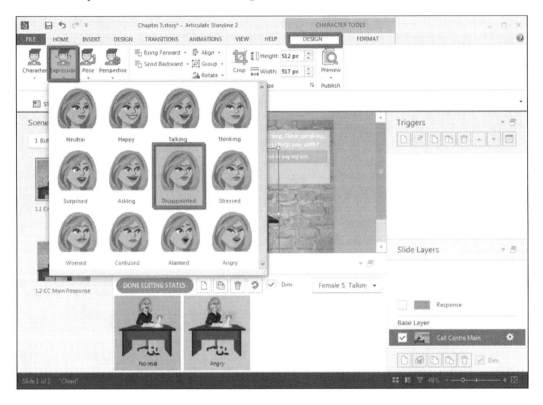

Deleting a state

To delete a state, all you need to do is select **Edit States** from the **States** panel, select the state you wish to delete, and click on the **Delete** icon. You will be prompted to confirm whether you want to delete the selected state, and once you confirm, the state will be removed:

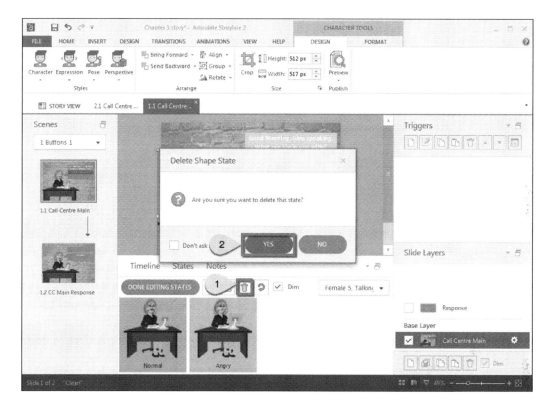

Specifying an initial state

Earlier, you learned that all objects will default to the **Normal** state. If you wish to start Gina off as **Angry**, you will need to change the initial state to **Angry**. To do this, select the **Initial State** drop-down menu from the **States** panel as highlighted in the following screenshot, and select the **Angry** state—it's as easy as that!

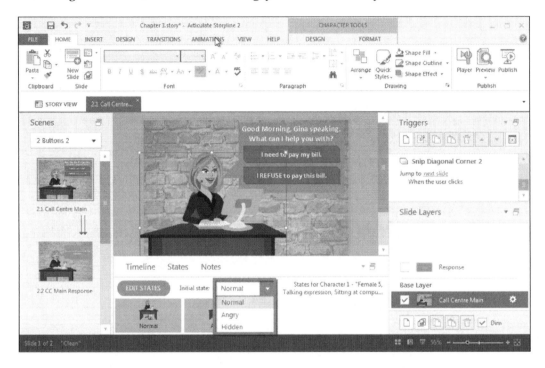

Making your states work

Built-in states (for example, button states) will automatically work; however, custom states, such as Gina's **Angry** expression, will need to have a trigger applied before it will work. This trigger will allow you to toggle between the available states.

For state triggers, you will add a new trigger, as previously discussed in the **Triggers** section, but when you select **Action**, you will want to select **Change state of** from **Trigger Actions**.

In this example, we will set the trigger to **Change state of** and our character to **Angry**, when the user clicks on **Button** indicating that they refuse to pay their bill. This will allow Gina to appear **Angry** when the customer indicates they need to pay their bill.

Once you confirm your trigger selection, you will notice that the **Change state of** trigger has been applied:

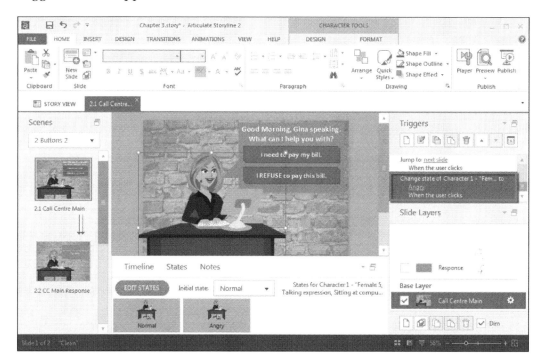

Using hotspots

Hotspots are a great way of creating button-style interactivity, and allow you to focus on smaller areas of a larger image or screen element so that the learner can interact with the smaller area as an individual element. Some of my favorite ways to use hotspots include:

- Creating custom navigation from graphics
- Revealing textual content on visual screens (for example, statistics on infographics)
- Showing zoomed in components without using Storyline's zoom function

Hotspots can help engage your audience by adding interactive elements to onscreen content and, when combined with layering, can truly maximize screen real estate.

When it comes to hotspots, the user will not physically see the hotspot in the published file. It will be invisible. However, you will be able to see the hotspot during development. As these objects appear invisible in the end product, it is recommended to use a prompt to guide your user through the interaction.

Adding hotspots

To add a hotspot use the following steps:

1. Select **Controls** from the **INSERT** tab. You can choose an oval, rectangle, or freeform hotspot. In this example, the arrows are a single graphic, and you will be adding hotspots to each arrow to make the single image behave as thought it were six independent arrow shapes:

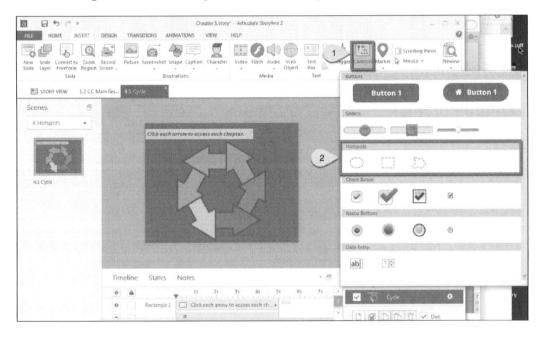

2. Once you have decided on the appropriate hotspot shape, you can draw your hotspot on the screen. You will notice two things: an opaque shape and an automatically populated trigger on the **Triggers** panel.

When it comes to choosing a hotspot shape, I would recommend basing your decision on the object for which you will be drawing around. In this example, the oval or freeform hotspot will work best due to the angles of the arrows on screen.

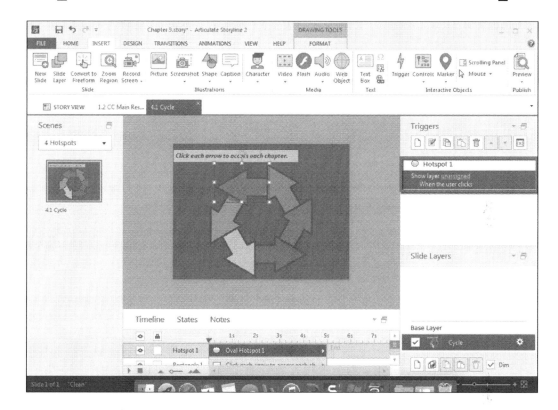

3. Once your hotspot is on the screen, you can resize it by dragging the arrows on the side of the hotspot. You can also move the hotspot around by dragging it to the desired onscreen location.

Adding a trigger

As previously stated, you will see that whenever you create a hotspot, a trigger is automatically generated. However, it defaults to a **Show Layer** trigger that is set to **unassigned**. To make your hotspot functional, you will need to edit the trigger. You will do this in the same manner you would any other trigger. Select the **Edit the selected trigger** icon as shown in the following screenshot, and dictate how you want the trigger to behave.

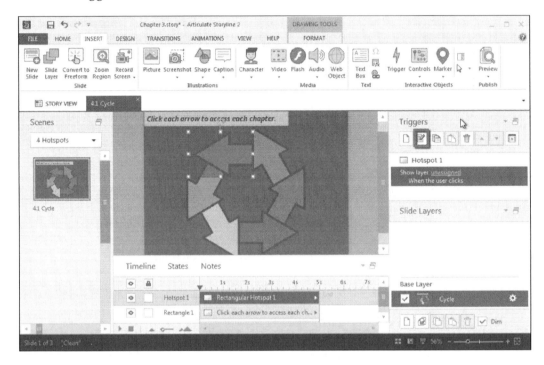

Summary

This chapter provided an explanation of the ways in which you can make your story come to life with more complex interactive elements: triggers, states, and hotspots. These Storyline functions allow you to take your storytelling one step forward and draw your audience in by having them do more and become active participants within your story.

Storyline has so many options for adding interactivity, and with triggers, states, and hotspots, you have endless opportunities to take your imagination to another level. Triggers are an essential function in Storyline, and states and hotspots make use of triggers. Now that you have a basic understanding of triggers, you should be ready for almost anything Storyline has to throw at you!

In the next chapter, you will learn how to make your story more realistic! You'll learn how to incorporate audio, video, and screen recordings. These elements will help your audience feel as though they are part of your course, and depending on how they're used, they may enhance overall engagement.

5
Making Your Story More Realistic

Now that you've learned how to increase interactivity within your story, you should be prepared to learn some easy ways of making your story come to life and seem more realistic to your audience. There are a few easy ways of doing this and this chapter explains how to make your stories come to life by incorporating audio, adding video, and recording webcam content to create a more realistic user experience.

In this chapter, we will be discussing the following topics:

- Ways to make your story more realistic
- Incorporating audio
- Recording audio narration
- Working with video
- Editing your video

Ways to make your story more realistic

Bringing your story to life involves giving it a real and tangible quality. For example, enhancing a visual dialog between two characters (for example, as in a comic book) by adding audio narration, bringing a nature-related scene to life with the background audio of chirping birds, or providing effective application simulations to effectively facilitate your student's learning of a complicated software program.

When these elements are added, the story will likely resonate more with your audience, making them feel as though they are in your story. Now that you've learned how to turn static content into interactive content, this chapter will take you another step forward by showing you how to easily create realistic and tangible learning experiences for your audience.

Incorporating audio

Adding audio is a way of easily injecting some personality or physical dialog into your story, and it can go a long way in helping to contextualize the story for your audience.

Finding audio can be the tricky part—you'll want to either create your own audio or source audio that is free to use in the public domain. This is important to ensure you don't run into any copyright issues (or lawsuits), and is especially important when your story is being used commercially or for profit.

Storyline supports various audio formats (AAC, AIF, AIFF, M4A, MP3, OGG, WAV, and WMA), and once you have sourced your audio, it's very easy to import audio into the slide you're working on.

To import audio files, select **Audio** from the **INSERT** tab, and then select **Audio from File**, as shown in the following screenshot:

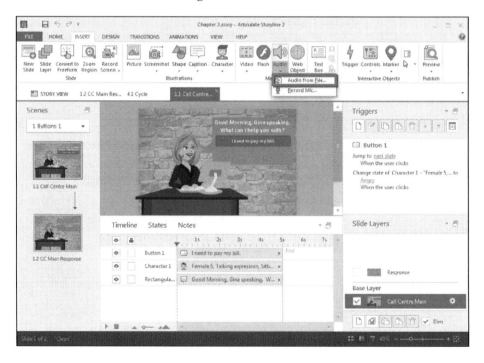

Look for the relevant audio file, and once selected click on **Open** and you will see your audio file appear on the timeline; when this audio file is selected, you will see an **OPTIONS** tab under **AUDIO TOOLS**:

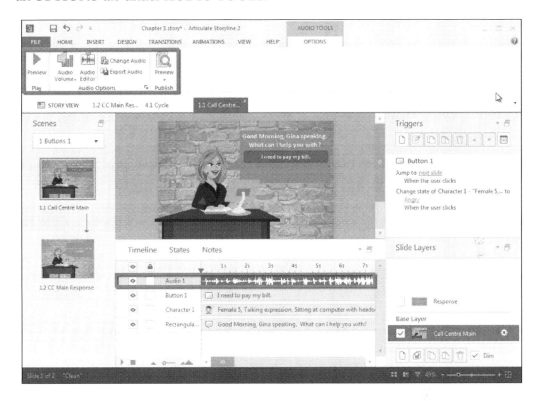

Within the **OPTIONS** tab, you are able to preview, adjust the volume, change the audio, export the audio, and edit the audio.

Audio Editor is a great tool and can be used to easily crop audio files instead of paying someone else to do it or instead having your voice-over artist re-record audio files.

To access **Audio Editor**, you have three options:

1. Double-click on the audio file on the timeline.

2. Right-click on the audio file on the timeline and select **Edit Audio**.

3. Right-click on the speaker icon to the left of your slide and select **Audio Editor**.

Using any of these options will call up **Audio Editor**. The following screenshot shows the **Audio Editor** window.

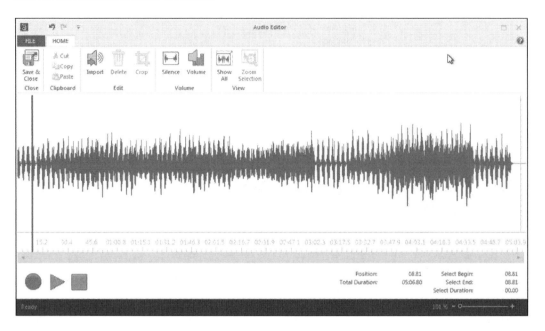

There are many functions within **Audio Editor**; however, only the basics will be discussed in this text. As such, you will learn how to:

- Crop audio files
- Delete sections from an audio file
- Insert silence into an audio file
- Adjust the volume of an audio file

Cropping audio files

Cropping audio files allows you to select a portion of the existing audio file that you want to keep, and delete the remaining audio in that file. To do this, left-click the audio track, in the **Audio Editor**, where you want your new audio file to begin and while still left-clicking drag until you reach the desired end point of your audio file. Then, select **Crop**, highlighted in the following screenshot. Anything not highlighted as a selection in blue will be removed from the audio file.

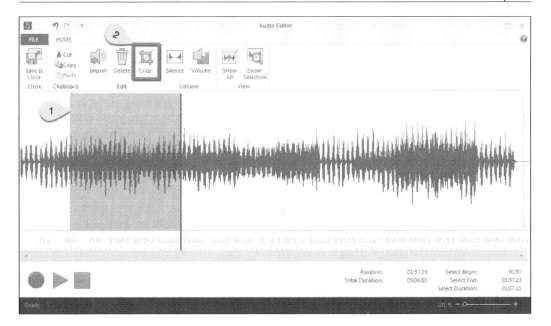

You will notice that your audio file has gone from being more than 5 minutes in length to being just over 1 minute in length, and you can use the playback controls to determine whether you need to crop any more of the audio file to achieve the desired outcome. The following screenshot shows the edited audio of 1 min length:

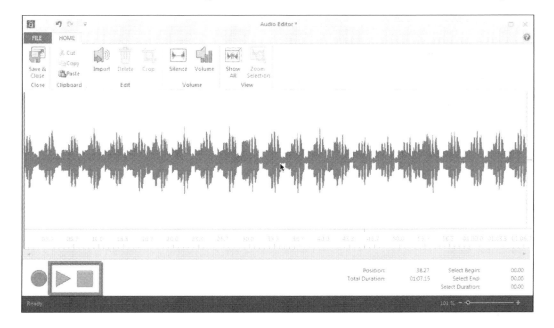

Deleting sections of audio files

Deleting sections of audio files allows you to delete a portion of the existing audio file. To do this, left-click the audio track, in the **Audio Editor**, starting at the location you want to begin removing and while still left-clicking drag until you reach the end of where the audio you wish to delete. Then, select **Delete**, highlighted in the following screenshot. Everything highlighted in blue will be removed from the audio file.

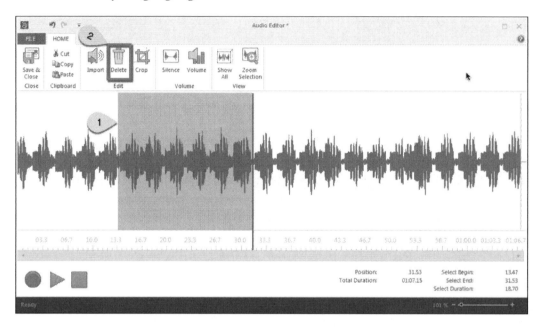

Inserting silence into an audio file

Inserting silence into an audio file is a great idea if you need to add conversational pauses. You want your learner to be able to listen to and synthesize the information they're hearing, and adding some silence can help.

To add silence to an audio file, select the area of the audio where you want to add silence and click on the **Silence** button. The **Insert Silence** dialog box will appear; here you will specify how much silence you want to insert. The following screenshot highlights the section which will be deleted:

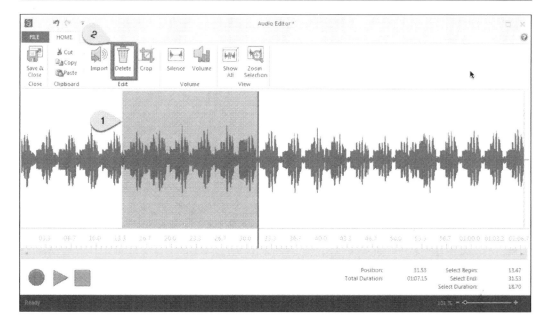

Once you've entered the amount (in seconds) of silence you want to insert into the audio file, click on **OK**. You will then see that 5 seconds of silence has been inserted into the audio file and is indicated by a section highlighted in blue:

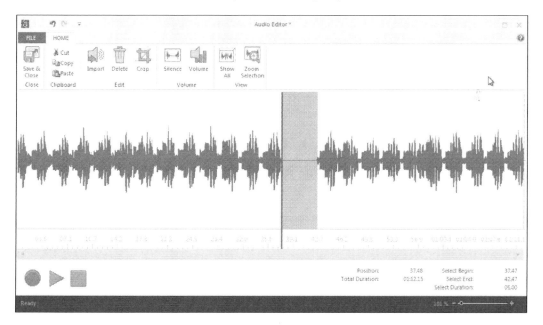

Adjusting the volume of an audio file

You might want to adjust the volume of your audio file to make it louder or quieter to ensure that the volume is at the desired level of loudness so that your users can focus on their training instead of fidgeting with the volume controls of your story.

Adjusting the volume of an audio file is simple! With **Audio Editor** open, select the **Volume** button. The **Change Volume** dialog box will appear, as highlighted in the following screenshot; here you can increase or decrease the audio file to the desired percentage, and when you're satisfied, click on **OK**. The specified volume will be applied to the audio file.

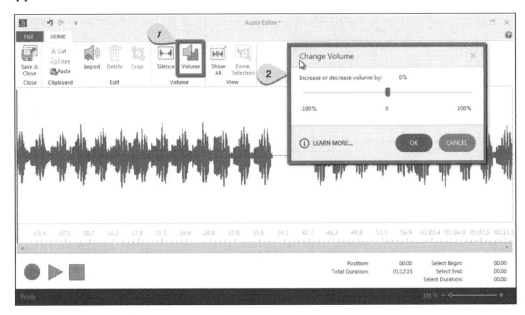

Recording audio narration

Recording audio narration is a great way to inject audio into our story without breaking the bank, as recording your own audio narration is often more cost-effective than sending it to a voice-over artist. This is also a great option if your client has a shoestring budget and can't afford to hire a voice-over artist.

Alternatively, recording your own audio narration can be helpful for use as *scratch audio*, or placeholder audio. For example, you might want your client to have the look/feel/sound of the big picture during their initial review, and adding the audio narration can be very helpful for your client in finalizing the script before you send it to a voice-over artist, and doing this can save you a lot of time and money (against your project budget)! Plus, it allows your client to base their review on a more realistic representation of the end product.

To record audio narration, select **Audio** from the **INSERT** tab, and select **Record Mic**:

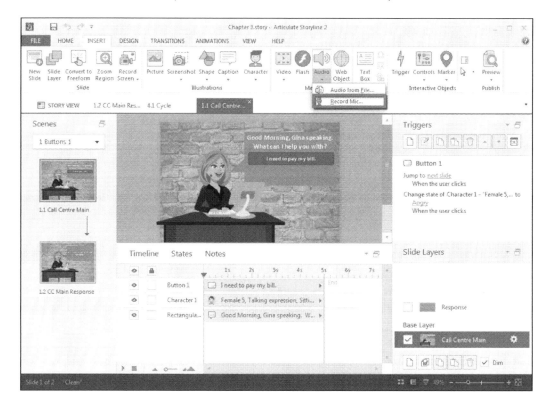

The **Record Microphone** screen will appear. Here, you will be able to record, play/pause, rewind, remove, edit, or import audio files:

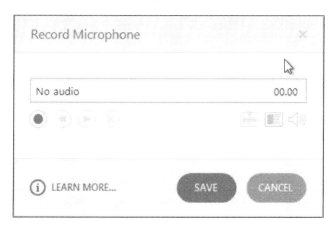

Another great feature of the **Record Microphone** menu is the narration script, and I realize that I'm mentioning this before I explain how to record narration, but it's something you should consider using before you record! The narration script function allows you to compose the text to be recorded, so that once you begin recording your narration, you can easily read from the narration script without having to toggle between Storyline and another script document. The following screenshot shows the **Record Microphone** menu.

To access the narration script, select the icon on the **Record Microphone** menu that looks like two panes (one for the text and one for an image). A **Narration Script** popup will appear, as shown in the following screenshot, and you can add the relevant narration script, selecting **CLOSE** once you have completed your recording and no longer need the narration script.

Alright—back to actually recording the narration. Once you have the **Record Microphone** screen open and are ready to begin recording your narration, click on the **Record** button highlighted in the following screenshot. A three-second countdown will occur, and your recording will begin once the countdown has finished.

Once you have finished recording your narration, select the stop button:

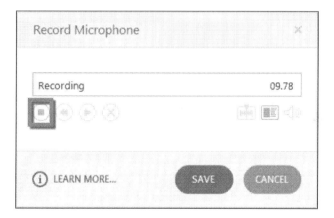

Using the play and rewind buttons, highlighted in the following screenshot, you can playback the recorded audio, and you can determine whether it's satisfactory.

Keep in mind that you can use **Audio Editor** to crop out any extended pauses, delete minor errors in the recording, or even add to the recording.

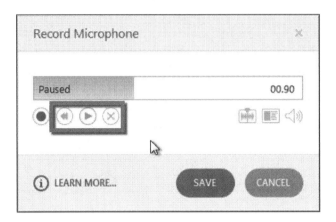

Adding videos

Video is a great way to enhance your e-learning project by offering another means of engaging your audience. It's always nice to break up text-based slides, no matter how interactive you've made them, every once in a while. Plus, people come from all walks of life when it comes to their learning styles, so adding video files can really go a long way at enhancing the learning experience for individuals who learn best from video-based courses.

As with audio, finding video files can sometimes be tough, and you'll want to make sure you aren't infringing on anyone's copyright, especially if your course will eventually be sold. Luckily, Storyline has some options for adding video, and one of those options allows you to create your own videos, using your webcam.

Within Storyline, you have three options to add video:

- **Video from File**
- **Video from Website**
- **Record Webcam**

To access these options, select **Video** from the I**NSERT** tab:

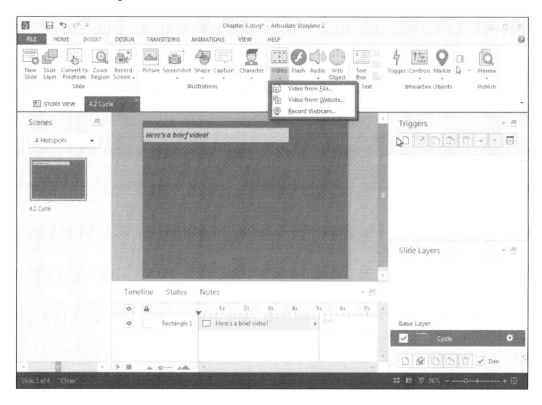

Adding a video from the file

To add a video from the file, select **Video from File** from the **Video** drop-down menu, look for the video file you wish to add, and select **Open**:

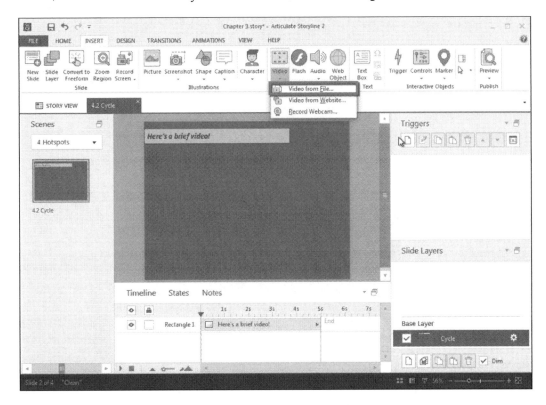

Storyline can support the following video files: FLV, MP4, SWF, 3G2, 3GP, ASF, AVI, DV, M1V, M2V, M4V, MOV, MPE, MPEG, MPG, QT, and WMV.

Once you select **Open**, you will see that your video file has been added to the slide, the video file appears on the timeline, and when the video is selected, you are presented with a **Video Tools Options** menu:

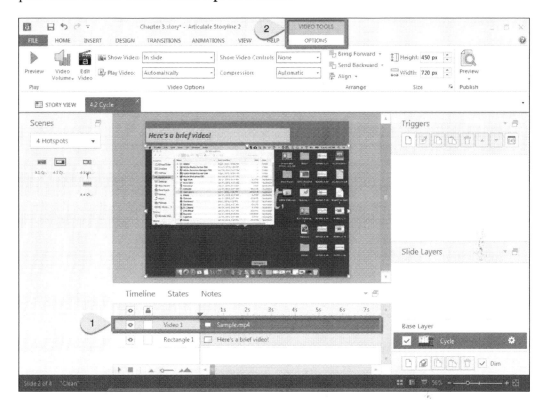

Within the **Video Tools Options** menu, you can adjust the video volume, edit the video (including trimming, cropping, adjusting the brightness or contrast, adding a logo, or even swapping the entire video out), change the size of the video, and dictate where the video will show when it is played, and whether it will include video controls.

Adding a video from the website

Adding video from a website allows you to stream the video content directly from the Internet; the caveat is that the user will require an Internet connection to access the embedded content.

To add a video from the website, select **Video from Website** from the **Video** drop-down menu:

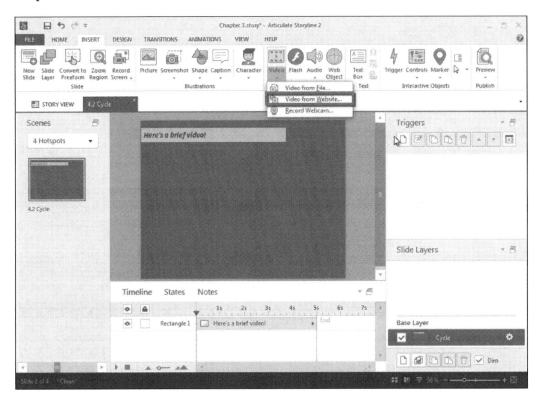

The **Insert Video from Website** window will appear. You will need to paste the embed code from the website video into the textbox.

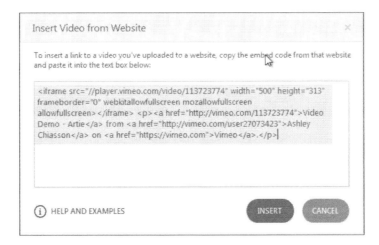

Once you have your embed code entered, select **INSERT** and your video will appear on the slide and on your timeline as an online video:

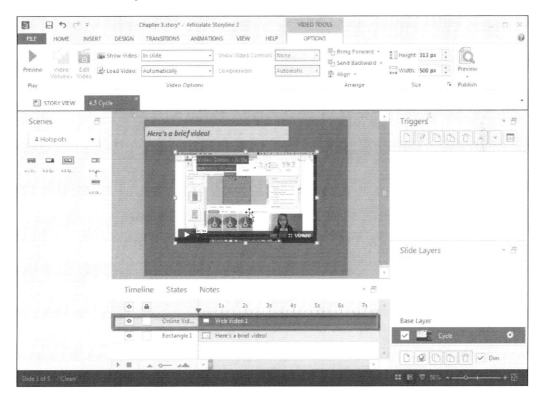

Recording a video from the webcam

To record a video from your webcam, select **Record Webcam** from the **Video** drop-down menu:

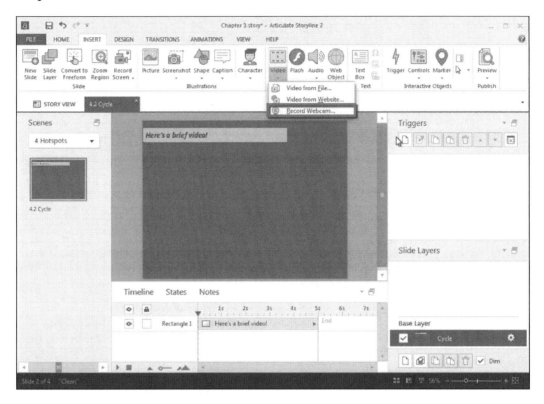

The **Record Webcam** window will appear, as shown in the following screenshot. To begin your recording, select the **Record** button. A three-second countdown will appear and your recording will begin once the countdown has finished.

Once recorded, you can playback your recording, stop the recording, or delete the recording using the available icons, highlighted in the following screenshot. If you are satisfied with the recording, you can select **OK**:

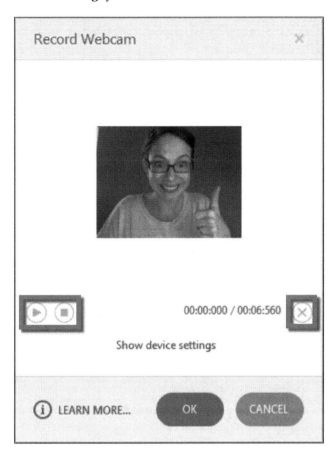

Once you've selected **OK**, your webcam recording will appear on your slide and on your timeline, as shown in the following screenshot.

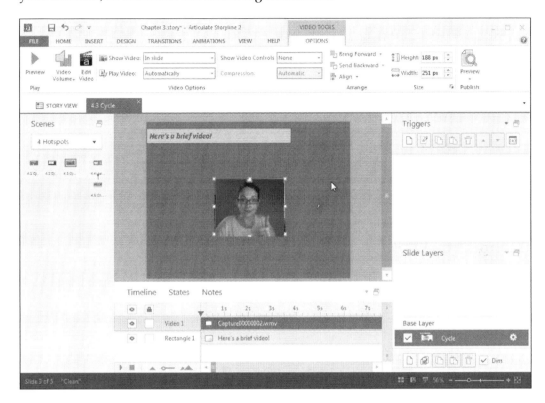

 You can change the settings for all videos you add, regardless of how they're added (for example, from a file, website, or webcam recording) using the **Video Tools Options** menu, as previously discussed.

Editing your video

Storyline lets you easily edit videos with the **Edit Video** feature. To access **Edit Video**, select your video and then choose **Edit Video** from the **Video Tools** menu highlighted in the following screenshot.

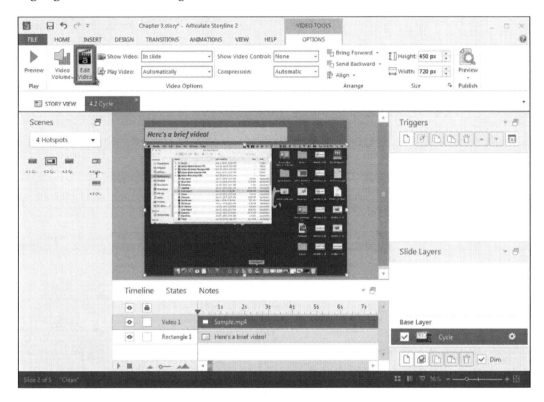

Articulate Video Editor will appear, and here you can trim, crop, adjust the volume/brightness/contrast, insert a logo, and change or reset the video. For the purpose of this book, you will learn how to trim and crop your video, as these features may be more complicated than others offered in **Articulate Video Editor**.

Trimming your video

Trimming videos is great when you only need to show a portion of the video. To trim the video, select the **Trim** button highlighted in the following screenshot and then drag the timeline to the desired start and end points. Once you have determined the appropriate start and end points, select the **Trim** button again, and your video will be trimmed. You will notice that **Trim Start**, **Trim End**, and **Trim Duration** are indicated in the video editor.

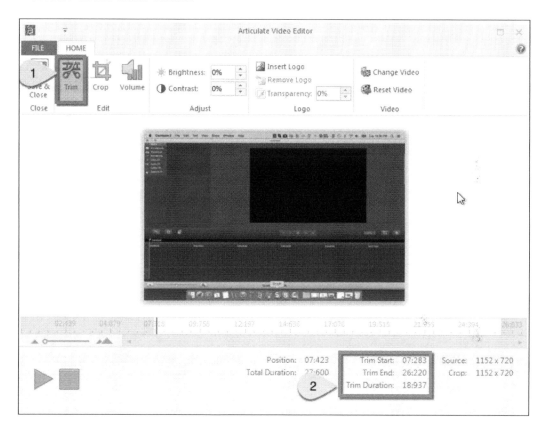

Cropping your video

Cropping videos allows you to adjust the height and width of your video, in essence allowing you to crop out elements you don't wish to see (for example, excessive white space). To crop the video, select the **Crop** button highlighted in the following screenshot and then drag the crop window to the desired height and width. Once you've determined the appropriate height and width of your video, select the **Crop** button again. You're video will be cropped to the specified height and width.

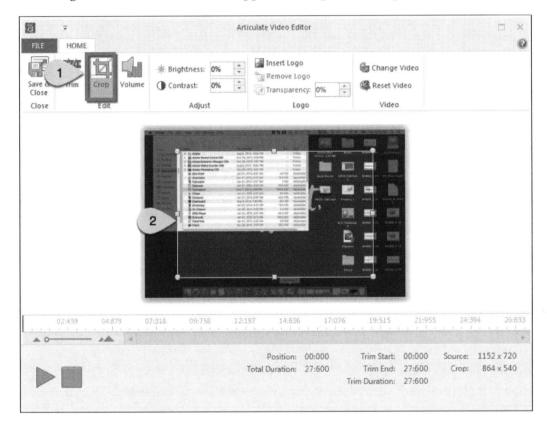

Summary

This chapter explained the ways in which you can make your story feel more realistic by incorporating audio and video elements. These elements can liven up your projects by adding a human quality, allowing your audience to feel as though they are part of your story.

If you want options for audio and video, Storyline has them! You can easily record audio narration, import preexisting audio or video files, import video from websites, and record your own webcam video. With so many options, you can take a varied approach within your story or you can pick and choose what works best for the story you're trying to tell.

Storyline has so many options for adding interactivity, and with triggers, states, and hotspots, you have endless opportunities to take your imagination to another level.

By now your story should be looking less like just words on paper and more like an elaborate story that engagingly describes whatever story you're trying to tell. Now that you've told your story, you'll probably want to assess your audience to see whether they were paying attention.

In the next chapter, I will show you how to test your audience. You'll learn about basic assessment concepts, all of Storyline's built-in question types, how to add and edit these questions, how to add a results slide, and how to use question banks. These elements will help you gauge whether your audience is actually learning the content you're testing them on, and will allow them to interact with your story in a new way.

6

Testing Your Learners

Now that you've learned how to create an interactive, engaging, and realistic story, you should be prepared to learn about how you can assess whether your audience has actually learned anything about the story. Storyline has a lot of options when it comes to developing assessment items, and in this chapter, we'll explore how you can use the available options to create meaningful questions that will test your learners' understanding.

In this chapter, we will discuss the following topics:

- Basic assessment concepts
- Question types
- Adding and editing questions
- Adding a results slide
- Using question banks

Basic assessment concepts

Assessment entails testing your learners to determine whether they understand the material that they have been presented with. Typically, courses include learning objectives. These objectives are used to guide the learner through the course, providing them with an expectation of their learning outcomes.

The two main concepts you should understand are that of formative and summative assessment:

- **Formative assessment**: This assessment occurs while the learner is progressing through the course. This type of assessment typically occurs as knowledge checks sprinkled throughout the e-learning project.

- **Summative assessment**: This assessment occurs at the end of the course and is designed to measure the learner's achievement of the learning objectives. For example, at the end of your course, you might include a graded quiz to determine whether the learner has passed or failed (based on your specified criterion and the learner's mastery of the content on which they were tested).

Question types

Storyline has 20 built-in question types that are all form-based. What this means is that you can select the appropriate question type and customize it by modifying the options presented to you in **Form View**. These questions take the guesswork out of building question slides, and can save you a lot of time. Within the **Quizzing** tab, you can see these question types appear under two headings: **Graded** and **Survey**.

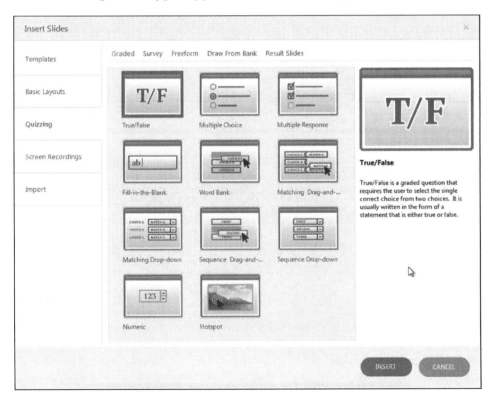

Built-in graded questions include the following:

- **True/False**: The user must select the correct answer from two options
- **Multiple Choice**: The user must select the correct answer from multiple options
- **Multiple Response**: The user must select the correct answer(s) from many options
- **Fill in the Blank**: The user must fill in the correct term/phrase to complete the question
- **Word Bank**: The user must drag the correct term into the empty box
- **Matching Drag and Drop**: The user must drag items from one column to match items in another column
- **Matching Drop-Down**: The user must select items from a drop-down menu to match column items
- **Sequence Drag and Drop**: The user must drag and drop items to arrange them in the appropriate order
- **Sequence Drop-Down**: The user must use the drop-down menus to arrange items in the appropriate order
- **Numeric**: The user must enter the correct numeric value
- **Hotspot**: The user must select the correct area within the image and/or screen

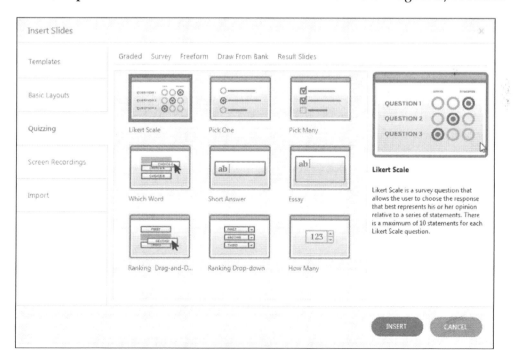

The built-in survey questions include:

- **Likert Scale**: The user must choose the response that best represents their own opinion
- **Pick One**: Similar to multiple choice, the user must select a single option
- **Pick Many**: The user can choose many options from a maximum of 10 choices
- **Which Word**: The user must drag and drop the word or option that best presents their opinion
- **Short Answer**: The user may enter a short response (up to 256 characters)
- **Essay**: The user may enter a long, essay-like response (up to 5,000 characters)
- **Ranking Drag and Drop**: The user must drag and drop options to rank them in order of the user's preference
- **Ranking Drop-Down**: The user must select options from drop-down menus to rank them in the user's sequential preference
- **How Many**: The user must enter a numeric response to the question posed

If time is not a concern, you might opt to create a freeform question. With freeform questions, you can choose from six interaction types and create your own question using any object on the screen. While this approach may be a bit more time consuming, it's a great option to step up your game and produce customized assessments that your clients won't see anywhere else! You can find these question types within the **Quizzing** tab under the **Freeform** heading.

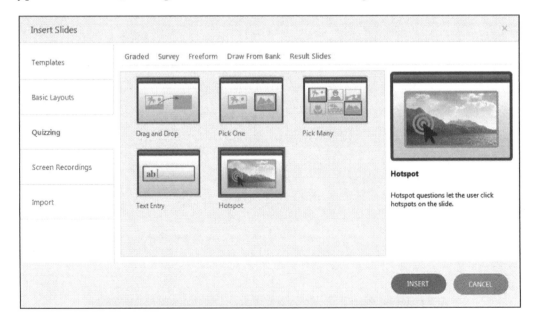

The built-in freeform questions include:

- **Drag and Drop**: This allows the users to drag shapes to set drop targets
- **Pick One**: This allows the users to select a shape, from multiple available shapes, as a correct answer
- **Pick Many**: This allows the users to select multiple shapes, from multiple available shapes, as correct answers
- **Text Entry**: This allows the users to enter their response in a text field
- **Hotspot**: This allows the users to click hotspots on the slide

Alternatively, you can convert any of your slides to a freeform assessment by selecting **Convert to Freeform** from the **Insert** tab:

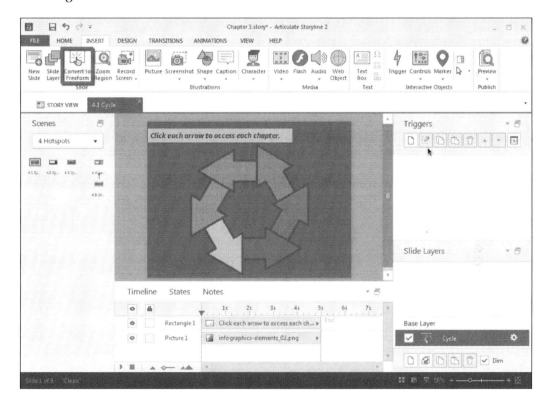

Adding and editing questions

Adding a question is easy! First we'll discuss adding form-based questions. Form-based questions are any of those contained within the **Graded** or **Survey** options, and they are named as such because you essentially customize them by filling in form fields.

From the **Insert** tab, select **New Slide**. Then, select **Quizzing**. Here you can select the appropriate **Graded** or **Survey** question type for your purposes.

 You can also use the shortcut key *Ctrl + M* to bring up the **Insert Slides** menu.

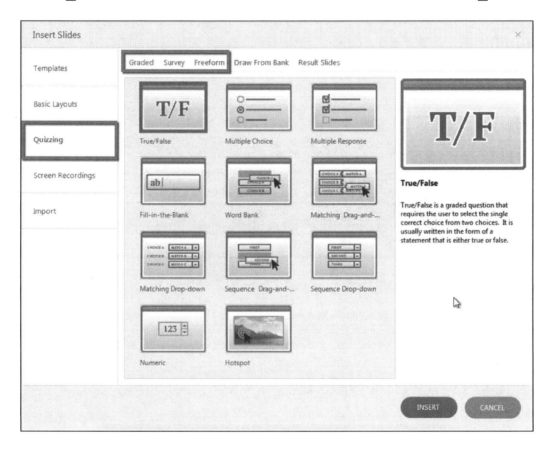

After selecting your question type, click on **Insert. Form View** will be displayed.

 Form View is a feature in Storyline 2; it allows you to toggle between the form view and slide view. In Storyline 1, once you select **Insert**, the question form will appear.

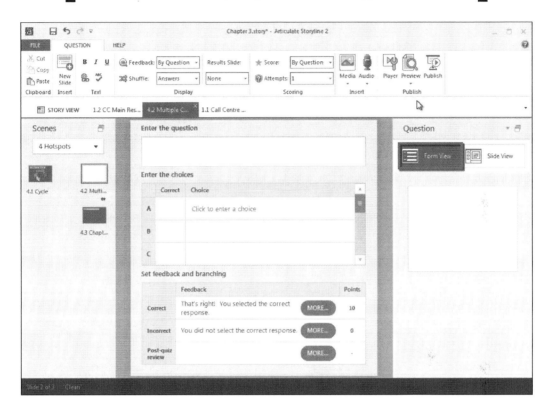

Once **Form View** is available, you will need to specify your question, choices, correct response, and feedback.

The **Points** column allows you to specify points per correct or incorrect response, and these points can be changed based on individual course requirements.

Type your question in the **Enter the question** field, type your choices in the **Enter the choices** field, specify the correct response by clicking on the correct choice in the **Correct** column, and enter your **Correct** and **Incorrect** feedback in the appropriate fields, or leave the canned feedback responses generated by Storyline. Once you are satisfied with your options, click on **Slide View**, and you will see how the question will appear in your course.

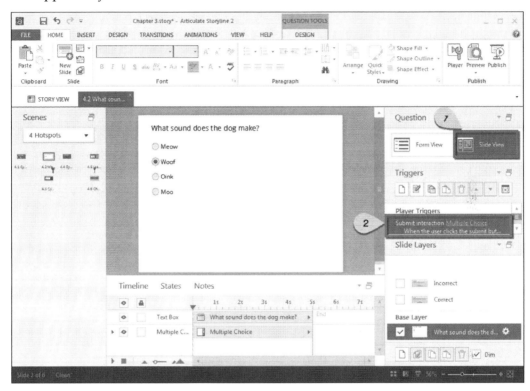

When you switch to **Slide View** or submit your form-based question, you will notice that there is a **Player Trigger** panel already set up to submit the interaction (in this case, **Multiple Choice**) when the user clicks on the **Submit** button. This functionality is fantastic because it helps automate the question-building process and streamlines your workflow.

Once the question slide has been populated with content, you can go ahead and make any technical adjustments using the **Question Tools Design** tab. This tab allows you to dictate when feedback will occur (for example, by question, by choice, or no feedback), shuffling (for example, by answers / not at all), whether there is a results slide associated with the question—more on that later—how the question is scored, and how many attempts the user gets to answer the question.

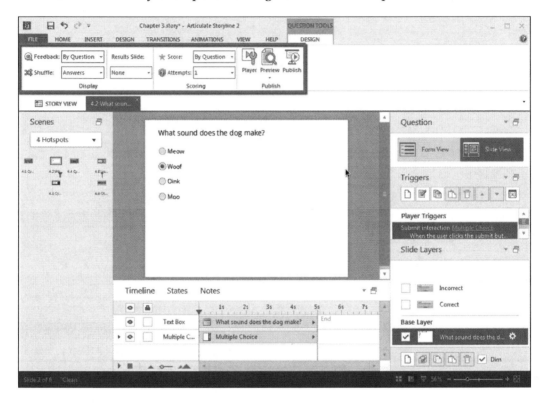

Now, you might be thinking that these slides look NOTHING like any of the other slides in my course. *It's so boring...* Not to worry! You can customize the elements of your question slides, just as you would any other slide.

For example, you can take that plain looking question slide, format the background, add some pictures as graphical elements, and shift around the question and choices text appropriately to end up with a very visually-pleasing question slide that has a similar design aesthetic to that of the other slides in your course.

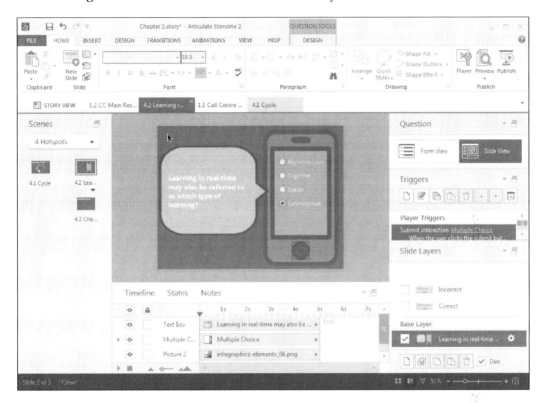

To leverage the aesthetic of your question slides, you really need to channel other basic formatting elements that you've learned in the previous chapters of this book. You're really only hindered by your imagination!

Now that you know how to add form-based questions, let's discuss how to add freeform questions. You can create freeform questions by modifying form-based questions to suit your aesthetic, but sometimes it's just easier to structure your design elements and then incorporate the assessment.

The first step in creating a freeform question is to layout your slide, including all of the elements necessary for the interaction. Once all of the interaction elements have been added, select **Convert to Freeform** from the **INSERT** tab.

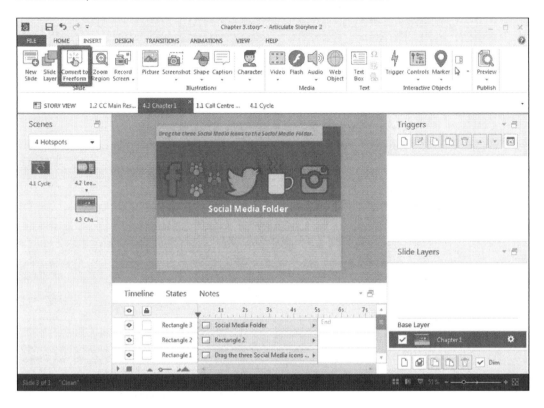

In this example, users will be required to drag three social media items to the social media folder. Once you select **Convert to Freeform**, you will be presented with the **Convert Slide to Freeform Question** menu, where you can choose the appropriate question type. In this example, we will select **Drag and Drop** and click on **OK**.

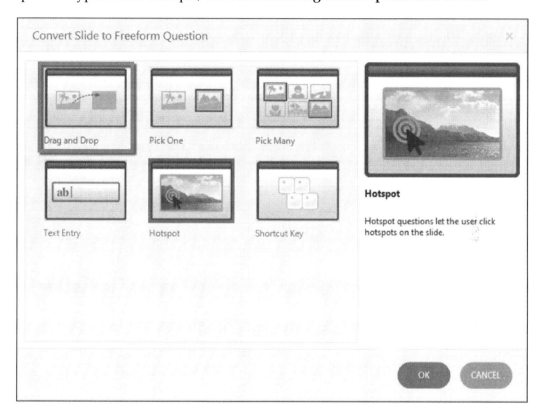

Once you make the question type selection, **Form View** will appear, and this is where you will define the **Drag items and drop targets**.

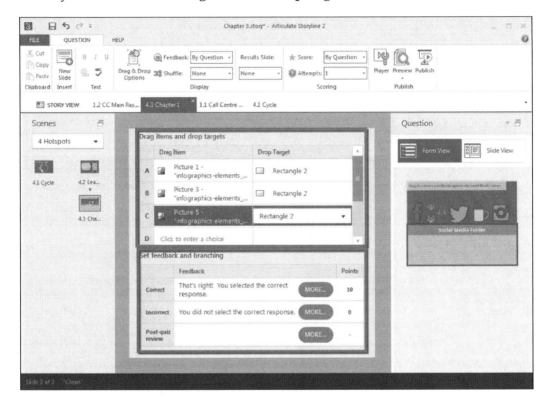

 On the right-hand side of **Form View**, you will see a small mock-up of the slide. When you select an option from the **Drag item and drop target** drop-down menus, the item you choose will be highlighted in red on the mock-up.

While in **Form View**, you can also customize your feedback or leave the feedback as the Storyline default, in the same manner you would with the form-based questions previously discussed.

Now, there is another way to add a freeform question, and that's by selecting **New Slide** and choosing **Freeform** from the **Quizzing** tab, in the same manner that you would add a **Graded** or **Survey** question. If you choose to add a freeform question in this way, once you choose the freeform question you wish to add and select **Insert**, the view will default to **Slide View** (versus **Form View**), and you will need to add the necessary objects for the interaction type.

It's an option, but you might find the first option of initially setting up your slide and then converting to freeform to be a much easier route.

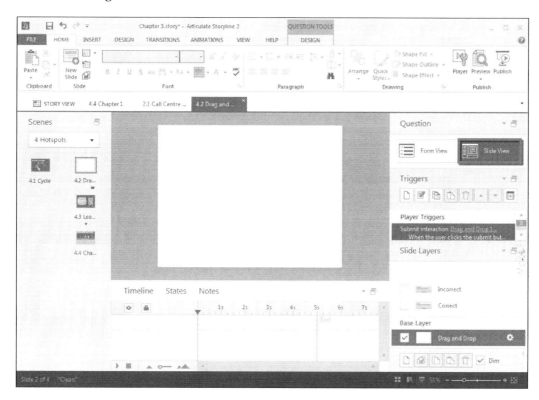

Using the **Convert to Freeform** option is also great because you can add all of the screen elements and then select the appropriate freeform interaction type, whereas adding a freeform question from the **New Slide** menu forces you to make the interaction type choice prior to laying out the slide. This isn't a huge deal—you can always change the interaction type at a later time, if necessary.

Please note that you can edit questions at any time simply by selecting the question you wish to edit and toggling to **Form View** to edit the question accordingly.

Adding a results slide

Results slides are used primarily for tracking course completion or progress in a **Learning Management System** (**LMS**). However, they can also be used to notify the user of their grade upon completing a quiz, or to thank the user for taking a survey.

To add a results slide, click on **New Slide** from the **Insert** tab, and from the **Quizzing** menu, select **Result Slides**. There are three options for result slides:

- **Graded Result Slide**: The user will be provided with a success or failure message, which is dictated by the user's graded score
- **Survey Result Slide**: The user will be thanked for completing the survey
- **Blank Result Slide**: This option produces a blank results slide

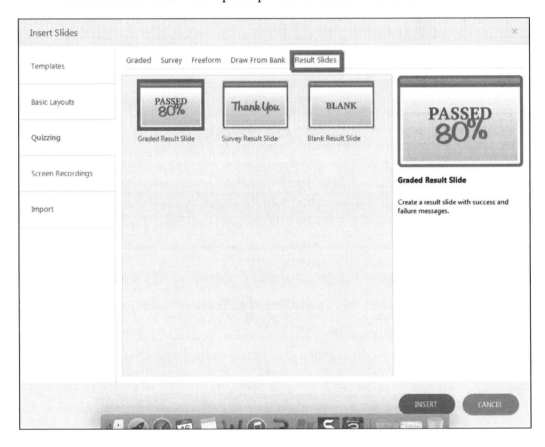

Once you have selected the appropriate results slide for your purposes, click on **Insert**. The **Results Slide Properties** menu will appear as shown in the following screenshot. This is where you can customize how the results slide tracks result. You will also dictate which questions the results slide will calculate results for.

 Knowledge checks or pop quizzes throughout the course may not need to be tracked; they may only be used for the purposes of reinforcing the learning objectives. However, you may have an end of course quiz wherein the results need to be calculated. In this case, you would want to ensure that the knowledge checks are deselected from the slides to calculate results for, and ensure that only the end of quiz questions are selected.

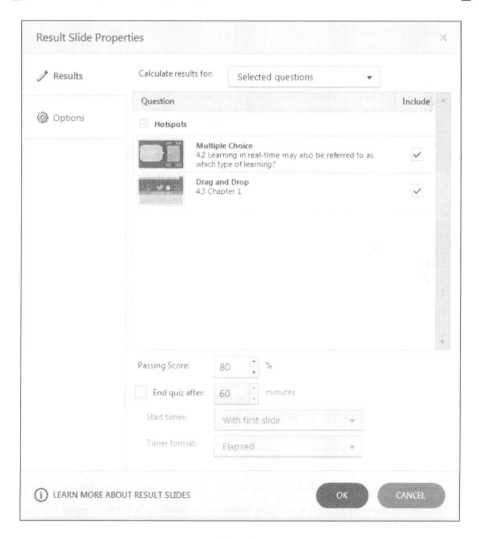

From the **Results** tab, which is the default tab of **Result Slide Properties**, you can also dictate a passing score percentage or whether you want the quiz to time out after a certain duration, and if so, when the timer will begin and what will be the timer format.

Selecting the **Options** tab will bring up additional settings:

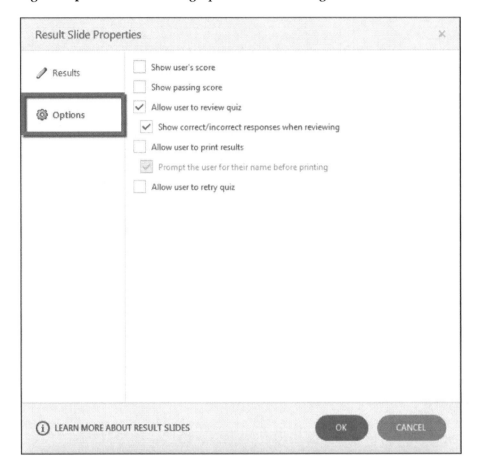

When you add a new results slide, the **Options** tab will apply two defaults: **Allow user to review quiz** and **Show correct/incorrect responses when reviewing**. Depending on how you want your results slide to appear, you may wish to deselect these defaults. Additional options include showing the user's score, showing the passing score, allowing the user to print their results, and allowing the user to retry the quiz.

The selections you make for your results slide ultimately depend on the requirements for your individual course, but you can select as many options as you'd like — you can select all of the options or none of the options; it's really up to you!

Using question banks

If you're developing a large course or just want to be supremely organized, then you'll want to use question banks! A question bank provides a storage facility for all of the questions within one course. Don't worry, you can pick and choose which questions go in the bank; once they're there, you can quickly pull them out of the bank and insert them or reuse them in your course as necessary.

To create a new question bank, you will need to return to **Story View**. Here you can select **Question Banks** and **Create Question Bank**.

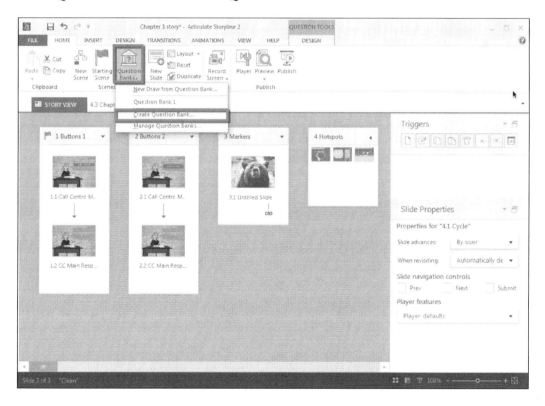

You will first be prompted to enter the name of your question bank. Once you do so, you will be presented with the **Question Bank** screen. Once you have questions within your Storyline project, you can choose to import them by adding them from the **Insert questions already in this project** prompt link.

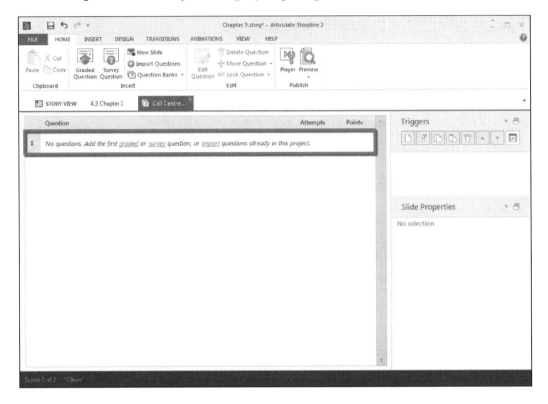

The **Import Questions** menu will appear, and you can select all questions you wish to add to your question bank.

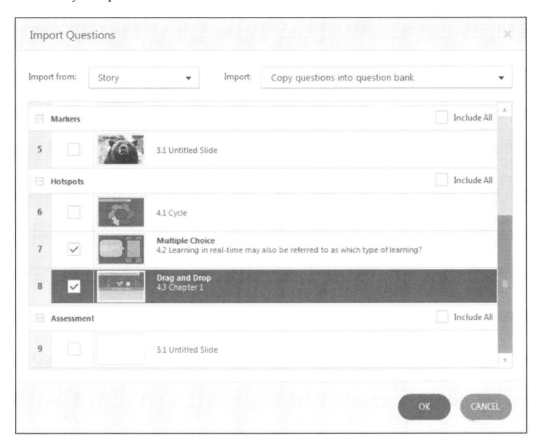

Once you have selected all the questions to add, select **OK**. You will see that they have been imported into your new question bank. Storyline couldn't make this any easier!

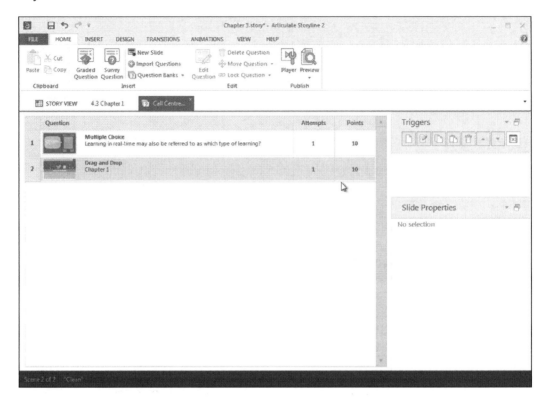

The **Question Bank** menu also provides all the necessary options for adding a new graded or survey question, adding a new slide, importing questions, loading other question banks, and editing, deleting, moving, or locking questions within the question bank.

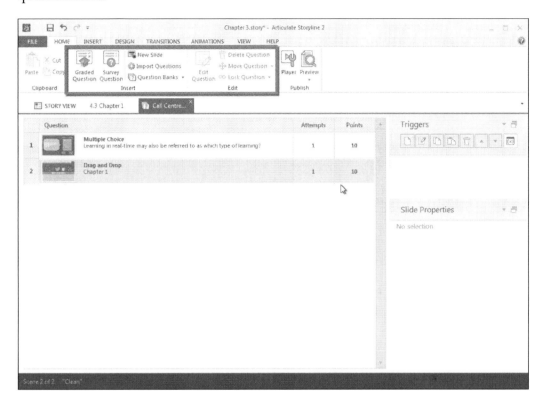

The question bank feature is one of my favorite features, and it will save you a lot of headache when working on larger projects that require reuse of questions or added organization!

Summary

This chapter explained some basic assessment concepts, which are important considerations when creating a quiz. For example, knowing the difference between formative and summative assessments may help you determine which quiz questions within your course you wish to have your results slide calculate.

Storyline really does make testing your learners a very easy process. With 20 built-in quiz questions, you don't need to feel hampered by a lack of creativity. However, if creativity is truly where you excel, you can easily customize the built-in questions to visually suit your course. If you're feeling an even bigger urge to empty your creative bank, you can work with freeform questions and create a truly custom user experience for your course.

You should now feel comfortable programming your results slides and setting your courses up for reusable content through the use of question banks. Throughout this chapter, you've learned about many of your assessment options, all essential elements in building a meaningful story.

In the next chapter, I will show you how to share your story! You'll learn about how to preview your story, customize basic elements of the Storyline default player, what all of those player properties mean, and how to publish your content, including the many options you have for publishing. This chapter will take everything you've learned in the previous chapters and will allow you to get your course in front of its audience. You'll see the fruits of your labor, and will be able to easily share your story with everyone else!

7
Sharing Your Story

Throughout this book, you have learned how to build an engaging and realistic story that will likely liven up the training experience for your audience. In order to reach your audience, you'll need to learn how to share your story.

Storyline has some great default player and publishing settings, but depending on the purposes of your course, you can customize the look and feel of your player and optimize your publishing settings as appropriate. We will explore most of these customization options and settings. Before you know it, your story will be in front of a live audience.

In this chapter, we will discuss the following topics:

- Previewing your story
- Exploring the player
- Publishing your content

Previewing your story

Previewing a story might sound like a straightforward concept, and it is, but Storyline gives you a ton of different previewing options, and you can pick and choose what works best for you!

There are two main ways for you to preview an entire story. The most straightforward way of previewing a story is to select the **Preview** button from the **Home** tab.

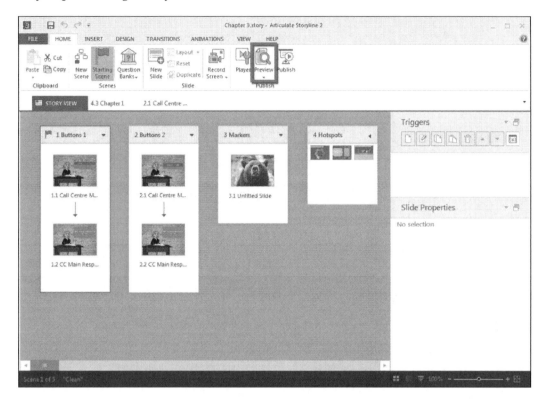

The other way to preview an entire story is to select the **Preview** icon on the bottom pane of the Storyline interface.

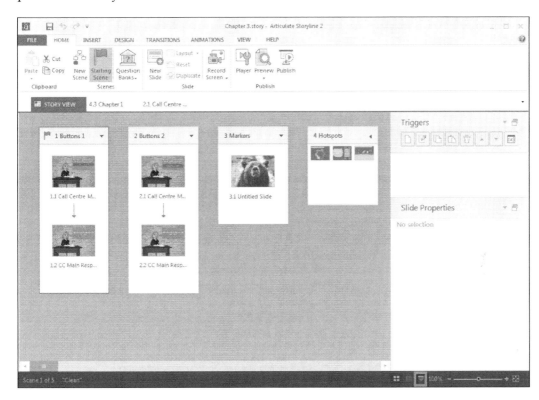

 You can also use the shortcut key *F12* to preview an entire story.

Once you choose to preview the full story, the **Preview** menu will appear. Here you can go through the story as your audience would and make any necessary adjustments prior to publishing the story.

Within the **Preview** menu, you can close the preview; select individual slides; replay a particular slide, scene, or the entire project; and edit an individual slide.

Maybe you only want to preview a particular slide or scene. In this instance, you'll want to select the drop-down icon on the **Preview** button on the **Home** tab, and then select whether you want to preview **This Slide** or **This Scene**.

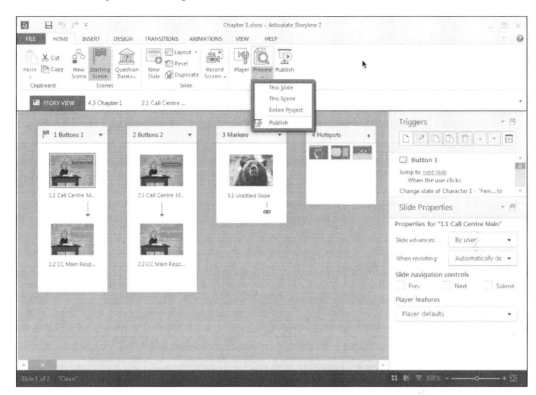

 To preview the selected slide, you can use the shortcut key *Ctrl + F12*. To preview the selected scene, you can use the shortcut key *Shift + F12*.

These options are fantastic and will save you a lot of preview-generating time, particularly when you have a slide- or scene-heavy story and don't want to go through the motions of previewing the entire story each and every time you wish to see a certain piece of the story.

It is important to note that not all content within Storyline is available during preview. These items include hyperlinks, imported interactions (for example, from Articulate Engage), web objects, videos from external websites, and course completion/tracking status.

Once you have selected **Preview**, you will be provided with the **Preview** menu. This menu allows you to do several things:

- Close the preview
- Select a different slide (if previewing the entire story or a scene)
- Replay the slide, scene, or entire course
- Edit the selected slide within **Slide View**

Once you have previewed your story and have determined that everything is as you want it to be, you're ready to customize your Storyline player and publish!

The player

The Storyline player is essentially the frame or shell for your course. It is highly customizable and can include features such as menus, resources, notes, and media controls, among many other features.

Storyline's default player is effective for almost any training situation, but if you want your story to stand out for your audience, you might consider some of the options for customizing the player. To access the player, select **Player** from the **Home** tab.

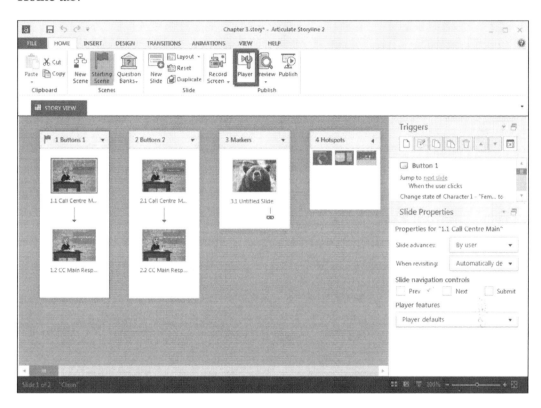

You will be presented with the **Player Properties** screen, and will notice that the player defaults to enable the **Resources** link in **Topbar Right**, the menu in the sidebar, the title on the left, and the **Volume** controls. You can see a preview of the selected **Player Properties** on the right-hand side of the **Player Properties** window.

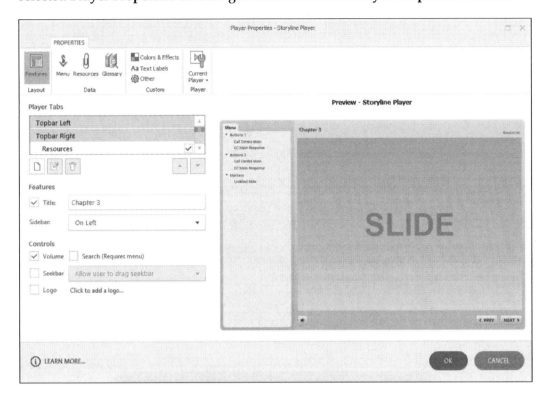

It is highly recommended to select and deselect all of the options to see exactly what they do. The preview on the right will show you what your selections have done, and you can always hit **CANCEL** and go back into the **Player Properties** if you've customized the player beyond belief and absolutely hate how it turned out.

Within the **Player Properties** screen, there is a **Properties** tab that allows you to customize various elements of the player. By default, you're taken to the **Features** tab. However, there are many more options available for customization!

You can change the position in which elements appear in the player using the up/down arrows and moving elements between **Topbar Left**, **Topbar Right**, and **Sidebar**. In the following screenshot, for example, the **Resources** element is located in **Topbar Right**:

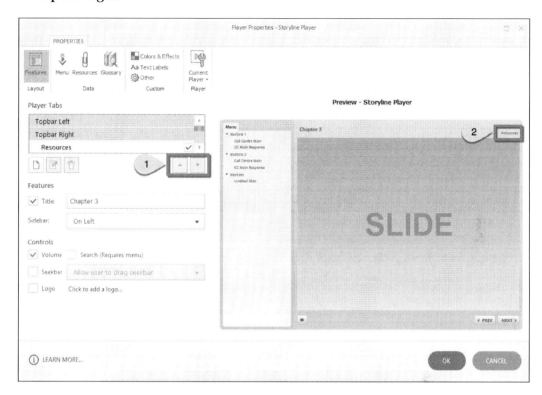

However, if you select **Resources** under **Topbar Right** and use the up arrow to move **Resources** to the **Topbar Left** player tab, you will notice that it moves accordingly.

The **Menu** tab allows you to customize the menu displayed in your player. Here, you can customize which slides appear in the menu (including adding and deleting slides or scenes), what they're labeled as, the order in which they appear, how they're indented, and how the menu functions. For example, is it locked or free? Are the menu items numbered? Will the menu autocollapse as the learner progresses? Only you can answer these questions, but Storyline can make your menu function just the way you need it to!

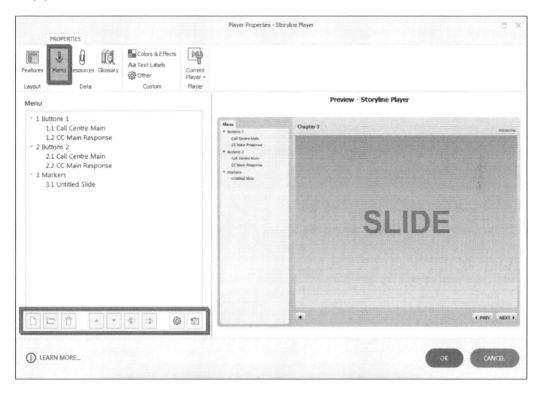

The **Resources** tab is where you can add supplemental resources for your story. You can use resources from existing files or from URLs. Here, you can customize the description given for your resources, add new resources, edit existing resources, delete resources, and change the order in which resources appear within the **Resources** menu.

Remember that the **Preview** pane on the right-hand side of **Preview Properties** will adjust based on any change you make, so you'll be able to see the cause and effect of your changes at any time.

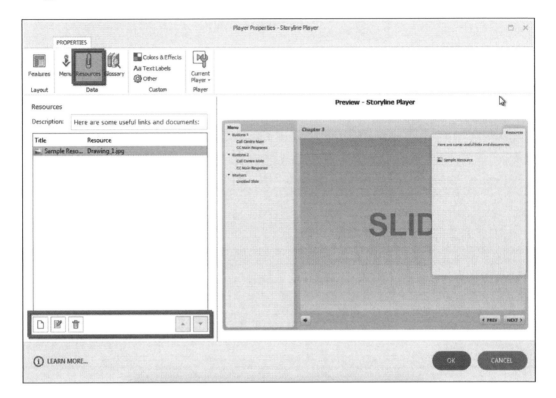

 The **Resource** menu is a great place to credit content that belongs to someone else but which appears in your course. It could act as a bibliography for your story!

The **Glossary** tab is not a default within the player. However, if you wish to include a **Glossary** in your story, you can select it from the **Features** tab. Within the **Glossary** tab, you can add, edit, delete, and change the position of glossary terms.

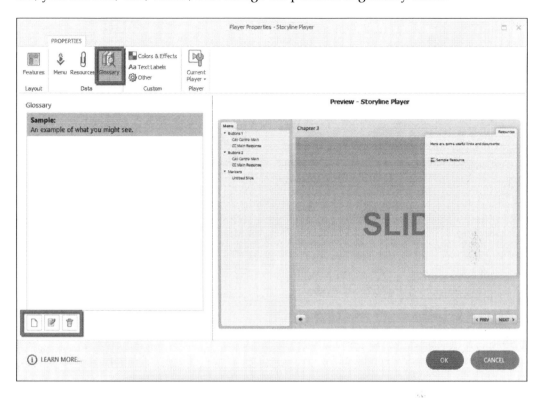

The **Colors & Effects** tab allows you to customize the color scheme, background page color, and player font. The only limitation here is your imagination.

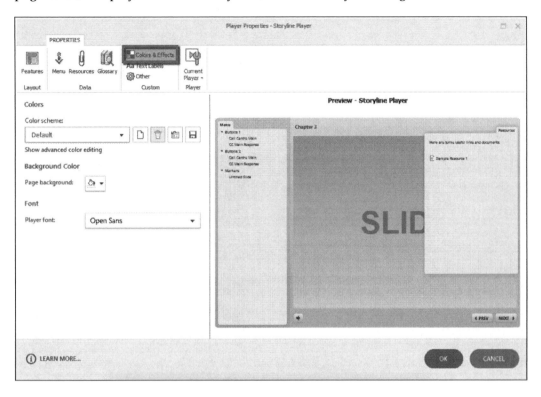

As for colors, Storyline 2 provides you with ten built-in color schemes, but you can also duplicate, delete, reset, and save color schemes. If the built-in color schemes don't suit the purposes of your story, you can select **Show advanced color editing**, and you will be provided with many more options to customize each element of the player. Again, the only limitation here is your imagination!

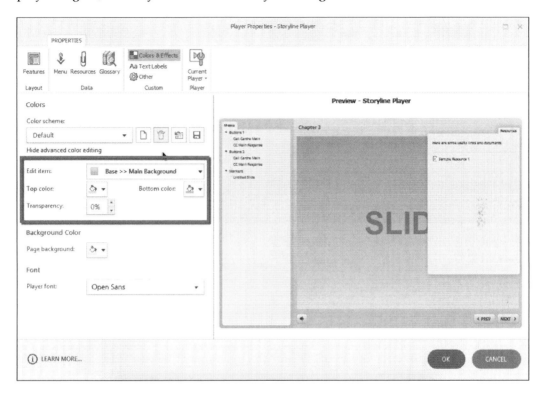

The default page background is white, but if you want to change the background color of your Storyline output, you can do so by selecting the **Page Background** drop-down menu and choosing the desired color.

Note that this selection does not change the actual player colors, it changes the background of the HTML page that is produced in your Storyline output. As you can see in the following example, the page background has been set to green while the player color scheme is set to the default grey. The **Preview** pane shows you what this will look like in the Storyline output.

Font allows you to easily change the font displayed throughout your player. Any text-related item in any of the **Player Properties** (for example, **Menu**, **Resources**, **Title**, and so on) will change from the default to whichever font you choose.

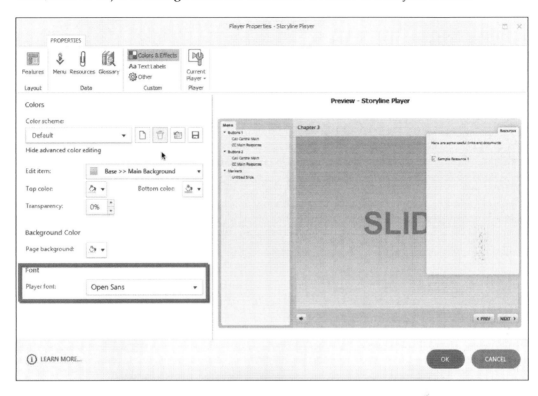

You can even customize the text labels that appear throughout your story. For example, if you had a list of course materials necessary for the completion of your course, you might opt to change the **Resources** tab to read **Course Materials**, and then contain all of your course materials within the **Resources** tab. Alternatively, you might want to include a transcript and make it obvious that this transcript exists. In this case, you might change the **Notes** tab to read transcript, and when users navigate to each screen, they can select the **Transcript** tab to read instead of listening to the content!

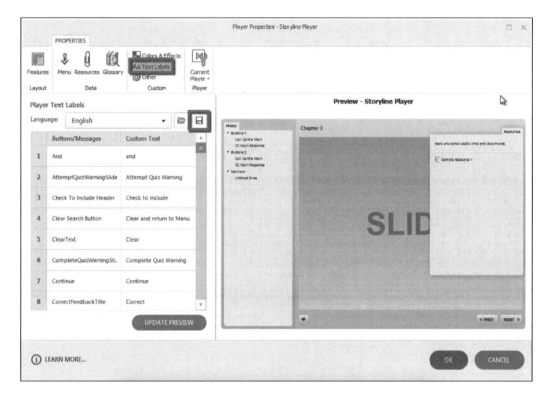

Once you have made all the relevant text label changes, ensure that you save these changes. When you select the **Save** icon, you will be prompted to enter a filename for the custom labels. Do so and click on **Save**. Once saved, you can load custom labels for reuse in other stories.

To view your custom label changes in the **Preview** pane, select **Update Preview**.

The **Other** tab allows you to dictate the browser and player size and define whether the player launches in a new window, and if so, whether it has browser controls / allows the user to resize the browser. You can also change the default **Resume** settings; this is great if you don't want your users to be prompted to resume each time they access the course. You can also define whether you want the text to be read left to right or vice versa.

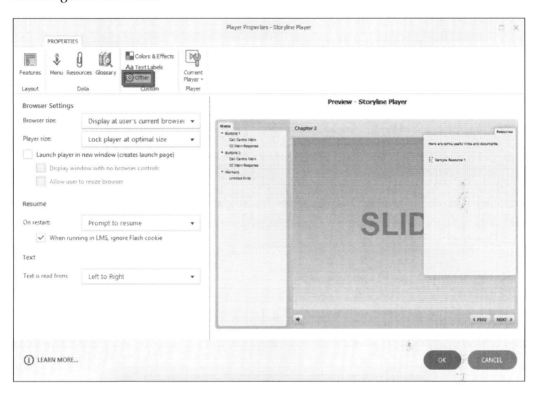

Once you've finished customizing the player, select **OK** beneath the **Preview** pane, and your **Player Properties** will be applied.

Publishing your content

Publishing your story is the last step in creating your very first Storyline project, except for revisions, of course. Now, Storyline provides you with five different **Publish** options, which might seem overwhelming; however, we're going to discuss each option at the end of this section so that you feel comfortable making the appropriate selection for publishing your story.

When you are ready to publish, select the **Publish** icon from the **Home** tab.

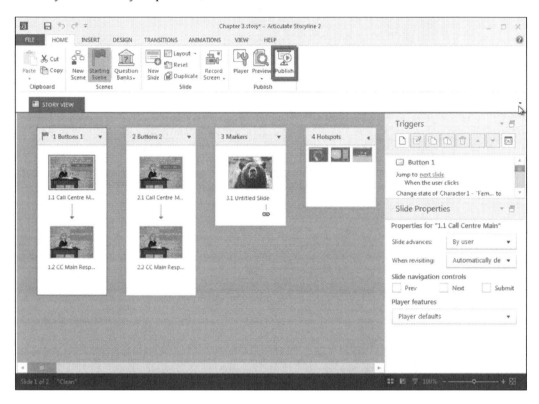

You'll be presented with the **Publish** menu, where you will see the five publishing options: **Web, Articulate Online, LMS, CD,** and **Word**.

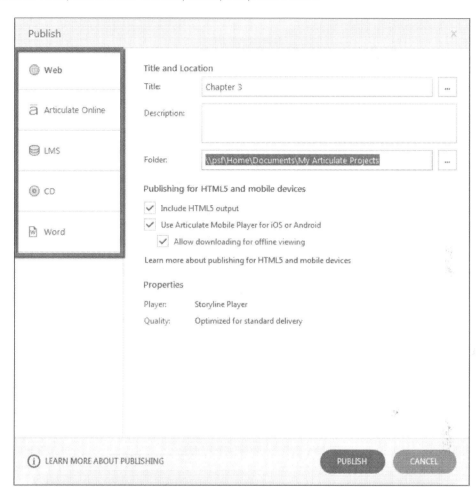

Storyline provides you with so many options for publishing your story, and it will take no time for you to learn which publishing option is right for you!

Publishing to the Web

Publishing to the Web is a popular option because it allows you to provide users with a standalone version of the course accessible online. However, if you choose to publish to the Web, you will be unable to track user progress or course completion. To publish to the Web, select the **Web** tab from the **Publish** menu.

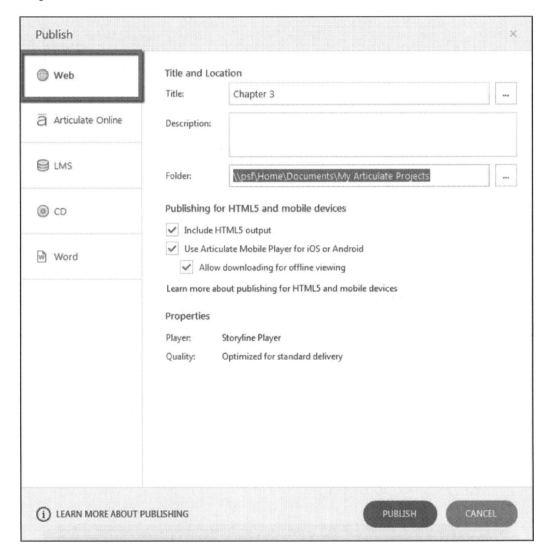

Before selecting **Publish**, you'll want to edit the **Title, Description**, and **Folder** location for accuracy. You can customize the publish settings if you'd like, but Storyline's defaults will get your course online quickly!

Once you select **Publish**, your course will begin processing, and once it has finished, the **Publish Successful** menu will appear as shown in the following screenshot:

We will briefly discuss the functions of each available option on this menu:

- **View Project**: This launches the published story in your web browser, allowing you to view the final Storyline output.

- **Email**: This opens an e-mail message with a compressed file of your Storyline output attached.

- **FTP**: This opens a window where you can use your FTP login credentials to transfer your Storyline output to the Web. This might be a desirable option if you're publishing to your personal domain.

- **Zip**: This creates a compressed file of your Storyline output.

- **Open**: This opens the folder where your Storyline output is contained.

- **HTML5**: This launches the HTML5 version of the story in your web browser.

If your courses require tracking capabilities but you don't have access to a **Learning Management System (LMS)** for testing and/or for distribution, you can subscribe to Articulate's Articulate Online service and avoid the hassle of having to deploy, manage, and maintain your own LMS.

Publishing to Articulate Online

To publish to Articulate Online, select the **Articulate Online** tab from the **Publish** menu, customize your settings to suit the needs of your course, and select **Publish**.

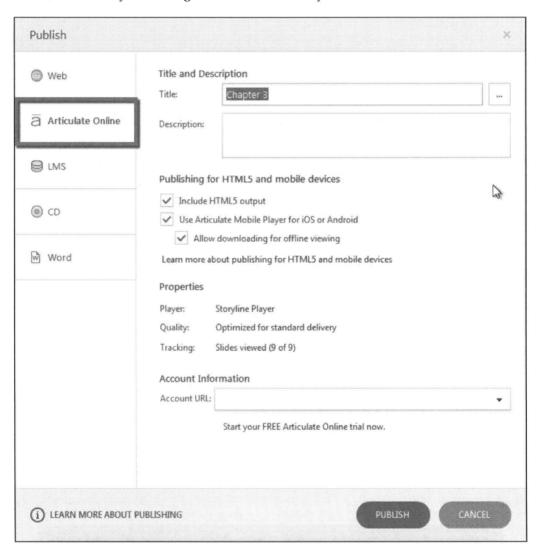

Your course content will be published to your Articulate Online account. The **Publish Successful** menu will provide you with one option: **Manage Content**; selecting this option will take you to your Articulate Online account where you can manage your content.

Publishing to LMS

Publishing to LMS is necessary if your course is going to be launched and tracked within an LMS. To publish for LMS, select the **LMS** tab from the **Publish** menu, make the appropriate selections to suit the needs of your story, and select **Publish**.

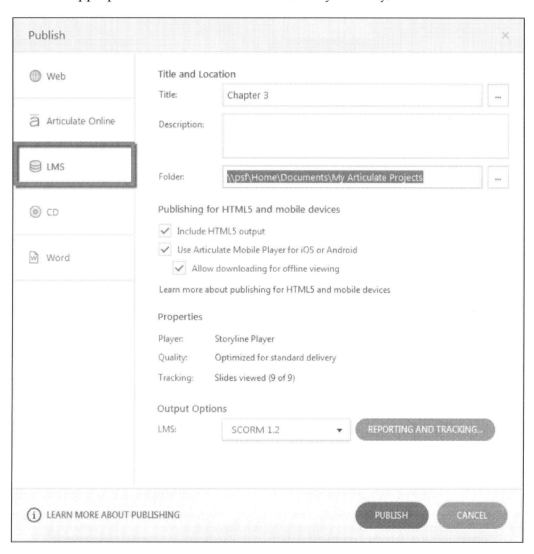

The **Publish Successful** menu will appear, and you will have all of the same options available, with the exception of **HTML5**.

Publishing to CD

Publishing to CD is a great option if you need to launch your course locally on a CD. You may also choose this option when completing the final delivery of a project so that the client has a hard copy of the Storyline output, or if the client works in a controlled goods industry (for example, the military) and requires access to hard copy standalone versions of the developed courses.

To publish to CD, select the **CD** tab from the **Publish** menu, customize the **Title**, **Description**, and the destination folder, and select **Publish**.

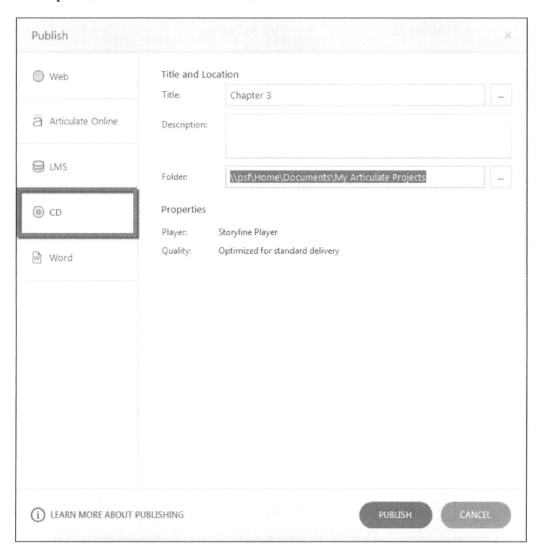

The **Publish Successful** menu will appear and you will be provided with the same options available as when you publish to **LMS** (for example, **EMAIL**, **FTP**, **Zip**, and **Open**).

Publishing to Word

Publishing to Microsoft Word is a fantastic option for creating a visual storyboard of your course. Internal and external reviewers can easily print, review, and mark-up this storyboard, and it makes the review cycle that much less painful!

To publish to Word, select **Word** from the **Publish** menu, customize the **Title**, **Description**, and destination folder, identify what should appear in the Word document, and select **Publish**.

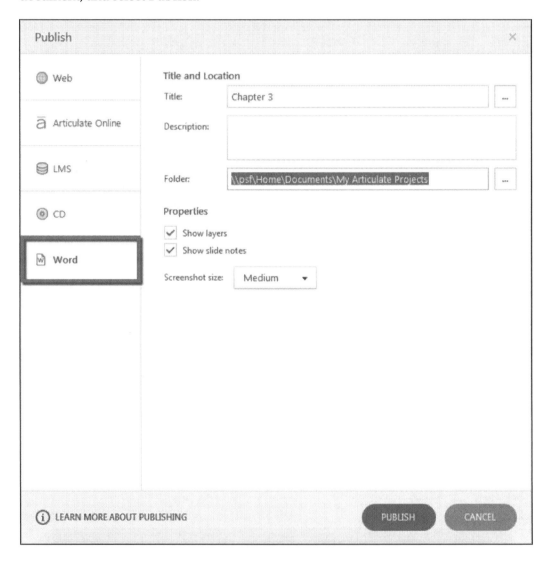

The **Publish Successful** menu will appear, and you will be provided with the same options available as when you publish to **LMS** and publish to **CD** (for example, **EMAIL**, **FTP**, **Zip**, and **Open**).

Now, there are plenty more options for customizing your publish settings, but the Storyline default selections will make sure your story is published effectively. As you gain more experience with Storyline, you can explore each option and customize your publish settings as necessary.

Summary

This chapter explained how to preview your story, customize the player, and publish your story. Storyline makes it easy to customize your learners' experience and share your story.

Previewing your story allows you to streamline your development; without a preview feature, you would have to publish every single time you wanted to see a slide — no one has time for that! You should now feel comfortable working with the player customization options, so let your imagination flow and create a custom player for your story! Publishing is important; it allows you to share your story with others, and you should now understand the purpose of each publish option, allowing you to publish your story for its target environment.

Throughout this book, you have learned how to become an engaging storyteller, enchanting audiences with dazzling interactions and realistic elements. You have learned all you need to know (and likely a bit more) to build out your very first story and publish it for all to see!

If you're looking to dig a bit deeper into Articulate Storyline's capabilities, please check out *Learning Articulate Storyline* by Stephanie Harnett, and stay tuned for *Mastering Articulate Storyline* by Ashley Chiasson (slated for release in mid 2015), where you'll learn all about pushing Storyline's features and functionality to the absolute limits!

Index

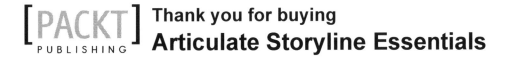

Thank you for buying
Articulate Storyline Essentials

About Packt Publishing

Packt, pronounced 'packed', published its first book, *Mastering phpMyAdmin for Effective MySQL Management*, in April 2004, and subsequently continued to specialize in publishing highly focused books on specific technologies and solutions.

Our books and publications share the experiences of your fellow IT professionals in adapting and customizing today's systems, applications, and frameworks. Our solution-based books give you the knowledge and power to customize the software and technologies you're using to get the job done. Packt books are more specific and less general than the IT books you have seen in the past. Our unique business model allows us to bring you more focused information, giving you more of what you need to know, and less of what you don't.

Packt is a modern yet unique publishing company that focuses on producing quality, cutting-edge books for communities of developers, administrators, and newbies alike. For more information, please visit our website at www.packtpub.com.

Writing for Packt

We welcome all inquiries from people who are interested in authoring. Book proposals should be sent to author@packtpub.com. If your book idea is still at an early stage and you would like to discuss it first before writing a formal book proposal, then please contact us; one of our commissioning editors will get in touch with you.

We're not just looking for published authors; if you have strong technical skills but no writing experience, our experienced editors can help you develop a writing career, or simply get some additional reward for your expertise.

Moodle Course Design Best Practices

ISBN: 978-1-78328-681-2   Paperback: 126 pages

Learn the best practices to design and develop interactive and highly effective Moodle courses

1. Explore Moodle's course development features like themes, social media plugins and archiving content.

2. Bring together instructional materials, social interaction, and student management functions in your courses.

3. An easy-to-follow guide to help you create or update your Moodle course.

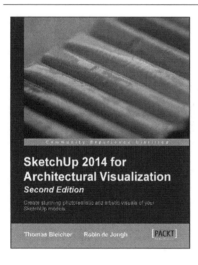

SketchUp 2014 for Architectural Visualization

Second Edition

ISBN: 978-1-78355-841-4   Paperback: 448 pages

Create stunning photorealistic and artistic visuals of your SketchUp models

1. Take advantage of the new features of SketchUp 2014.

2. Create picture-perfect photo-realistic 3D architectural renders for your SketchUp models.

3. Post-process SketchUp output to create digital watercolor and pencil art.

4. Make the most of SketchUp with the best plugins and add-on software to enhance your models.

Please check **www.PacktPub.com** for information on our titles

Designing Moodle
Themes

Susan Smith Nash

Designing Moodle Themes [Video]

ISBN: 978-1-78328-601-0   Duration: 02:48 hours

Effortlessly design attractive and functional themes for your Moodle course

1.   Create your own Moodle skin by customizing Themes in Moodle.

2.   Boost the learner experience on all platforms, from desktops to tablets and smartphones.

3.   Enhance the functionality of your Moodle courses through these quick, easy-to-follow, and engaging videos.

3D Printing with
SketchUp

Real-world case studies to help you design models in SketchUp for 3D printing on anything ranging from the smallest desktop machines to the largest industrial 3D printers

Marcus Ritland

3D Printing with SketchUp

ISBN: 978-1-78328-457-3   Paperback: 136 pages

Real-world case studies to help you design models in SketchUp for 3D printing on anything ranging from the smallest desktop machines to the largest industrial 3D printers

1.   Learn how to design beautiful architectural models that will print on any 3D printer.

2.   Packed with clearly illustrated examples to show you just how to design for 3D printing.

3.   Discover the essential extensions and companion programs for 3D printing your models.

Please check **www.PacktPub.com** for information on our titles

50732848R00101